Scroll Saw Projects

BY DONALD R. BRANN

Library of Congress Card No. 75-3911

Published by
DIRECTIONS SIMPLIFIED, INC.

Division of
EASI-BILD PATTERN CO., INC.
Briarcliff Manor, N.Y. 10510

FIRST PRINTING – 1975

A BETTER WAY

Those who invest a few moments to reflect on today's way of life, invariably reach the same conclusion. It's much too fast — there must be a better way. And there is. To slow down the hours of each day that still belong to you, develop a spare time activity that insures escape from tension.

Consider yourself two people with two completely separate spheres of responsibility. The time devoted to your business belongs to those who buy it; the hours outside still belong to you. Invest this time in handicrafts and you will learn to live a pace comparable to Colonial times.

Read through this book. Discover how a scroll or coping saw, plus full size patterns simplify building the many projects offered. Parents should encourage a child to build one or all. Those too young to work without supervision should be encouraged to help even if it's only to sandpaper a part. Showing a youngster how to turn a piece of wood into a useful wall shelf etches a constructive impression on the child's mind.

The step-by-step direction and full size patterns take the fear and mystery out of woodworking. Each shows amateurs how to build like a pro. Each requires time to build, time to relax and a better way to live.

Don R. Brann

TABLE OF CONTENTS

10 — Cobbler's Bench Sewing Kit

17 — Cigarette and Match Cradle

23 — Combination Plant and String Holder

28 — Fern Scroll Saw Shelf

34 — Colonial Planter

39 — Pony Book Ends

44 — Waddling Willie Pull Toy

50 — Wren House

56 — Mary and Lamb Wall Plaque

66 — Applique Shelf

71 — Lawn Ornaments

82 — Pony Pull Toy and Planter

87 — Door Stops

91 — Pierre The Potholder's Holder

97 — Name Plates

103 — Indian Wall Plaque

110 — Barnyard Pull Toys

IT'S EASY WHEN YOU KNOW HOW

The full size patterns in this book offer the reader a form of spare time insurance. It usually transforms Mr. All Thumbs into a craftsman on his first attempt. Tracing each pattern simplifies duplicating the original. If you want to keep the book intact, use carbon paper and trace the full size patterns on heavy paper, or zerox each page. Next cut each along the outside lines.

If you want to teach a group of children, retardees or the blind, transfer the paper pattern onto ⅛″ hardboard, sheet aluminum or ³⁄₁₆″ plywood. Cut these to exact shape. These templates can be used continually. Start with the easiest projects like those on pages 17, 34, 50.

Show a blind person how to trace an outline using an 8 or 10 penny finishing nail. This permits feeling the shape of the drawn outline. When a blind person begins to develop confidence, and wants to help others who are also blind, show them how to use an engraving tool, Illus. 1, to draw outlines.

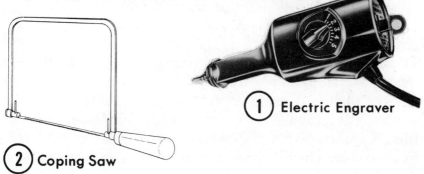

① Electric Engraver

② Coping Saw

Always start beginners with a coping saw, Illus. 2. They can be graduated to the sabre saw, Illus. 3, as quickly as they show ability. Adults who plan on making a quantity of any item for a church fund raising bazaar, or plan on helping a Boy Scout or Junior Achievement group go into business, will find a motorized scroll saw, Illus. 4, and attachments, Illus. 5, a fast way to increase production. Always drill a ¼ or ⅜″ pilot hole where a saw requires same.

To simplify teaching the very young, retardees, or the blind, use the actual parts of each project. When teaching the blind, number each part using an engraving tool, Illus. 1. Use large numerals or letters. Next make up a set of preassembled parts, Illus. 6. Fasten part A to C so those who can see, quickly visualize assembly. The blind feel the shape of A, and visualize position of A fastened to C, etc. A complete set of preassembled parts generates confidence among the very young and is particularly helpful to retardees.

One way you can help even the slowest student is to make up oversize patterns. Encourage them to cut each shape to size of pattern to compensate for any error. By allowing each part to be sanded or sawed to exact shape required, you create confidence while you eliminate any feeling of shame caused by inaccurately cutting a part.

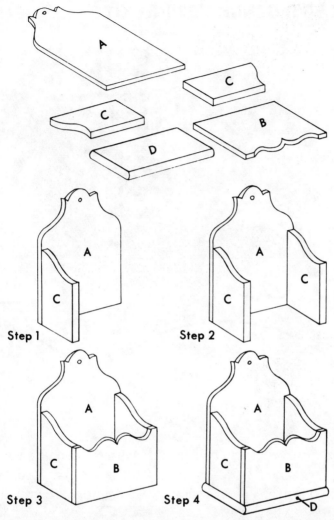

Step 1

Step 2

Step 3

Step 4

Building even the smallest and simplest project builds the individual. Scroll saw projects are especially important because they are great ego builders. You develop a child's self confidence fast when you teach him to work with his hands. Always mention what Joe built at every opportunity. Always suggest he or she build something that can be given as a gift to some relative who you know will help play the ego building game. A case in point is this miniature Cobbler's Bench Sewing Kit, Illus. 7. While an adult will find this project a real challenge, it's one that will generate many sincere compliments. It's also a project a youngster can build once they practice on the easier projects.

COBBLER'S BENCH SEWING KIT

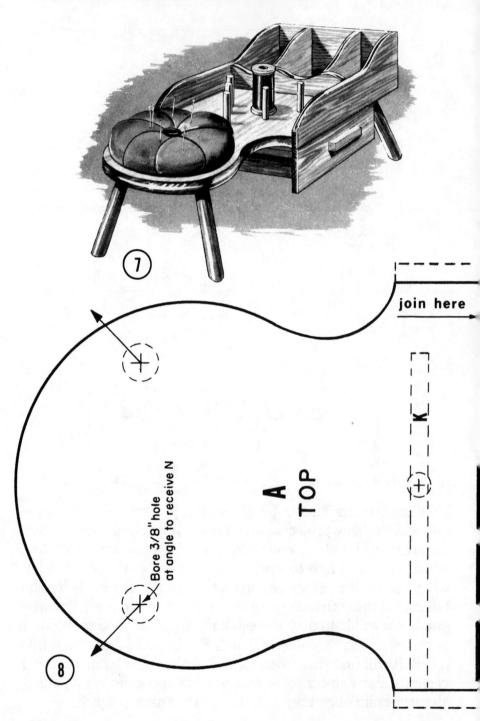

⑦

join here

K

A
TOP

Bore 3/8" hole
at angle to receive N

⑧

LIST OF MATERIALS

1 — ½ x 5 x 10″ for A
1 — ¼ x 4 x 24″ ″ B, C, D, E, F, G, H, J, K, L, M, N, O
¼″ dowel — 10″
⅜″ dowel — 12″
⅜, ½, ¾″ brads
glue

The solid black outside line indicates the full size of the part. Draw up a full size pattern by joining parts A together. The dash lines indicate position of adjoining part. For greater strength apply glue before nailing. Use ½″ brads unless another size is specified.

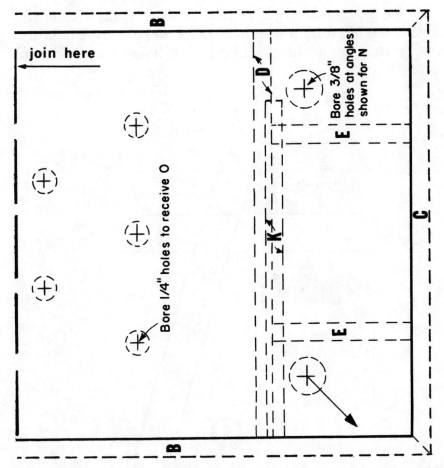

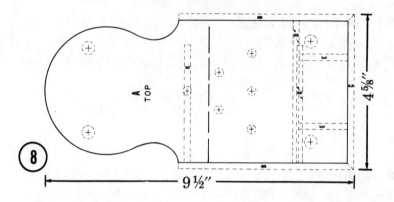

Cut top A to shape of pattern, Illus. 8, from ½″ stock. Drill five ¼″ holes in position indicated to receive dowels O. These act as spool holders.

Cut a leg hole guide block, Illus. 9, from 1″ scrap. Clamp the guide block in position where ⅜″ holes on pattern A indicate. Rest ⅜″ drill against block and drill four holes at angle shown.

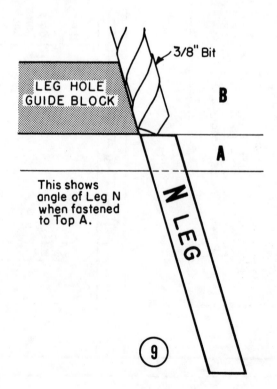

Cut two sides B, Illus. 10; one end C, Illus. 11; one D, Illus. 12; two E, Illus. 13; from ¼" stock. Bevel end of B and C to shape shown. Glue and nail B and C to A in position indicated; B to C; B to D; A to D; D and C to E, Illus. 8.

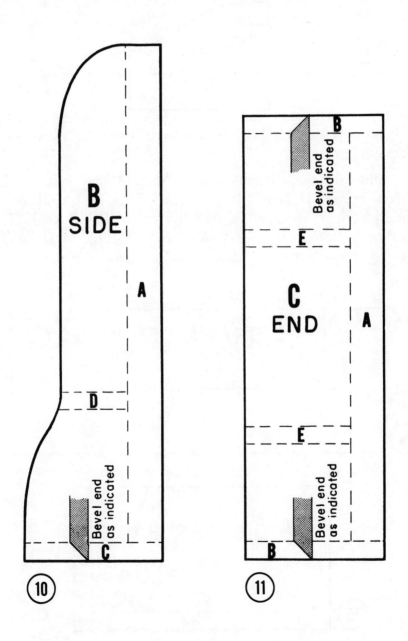

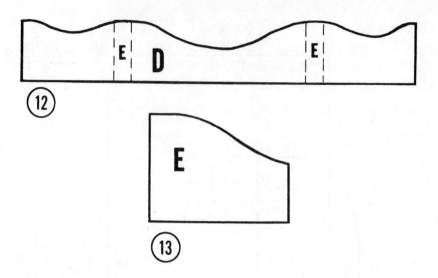

(12)

(13)

To build a drawer, cut one front F, Illus. 14; one back G, Illus. 15; one bottom H, Illus. 16; two sides J, Illus. 17; four K, two L, one M from ¼″ stock, Illus. 18. Glue and nail F, G, to J, H; in position indicated, Illus. 16. Fasten K to J, Illus. 14, using glue and ⅜″ brads. Cut six ¼″ dowels O, Illus. 18.

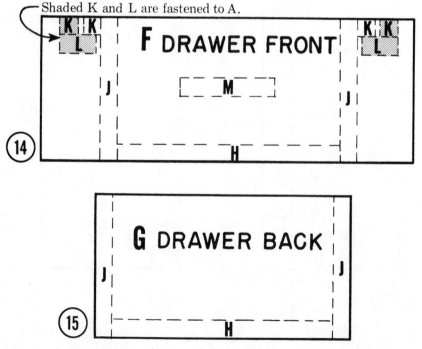

Shaded K and L are fastened to A.

K K
L
F DRAWER FRONT
M
J
K K
L
J

(14)
H

G DRAWER BACK
J
J

(15)
H

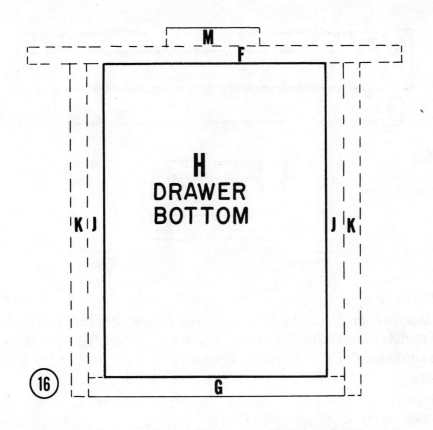

**H
DRAWER
BOTTOM**

M

F

K J

J K

16

G

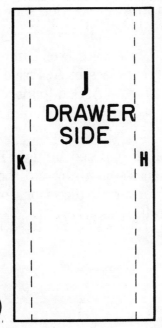

**J
DRAWER
SIDE**

K

H

17

15

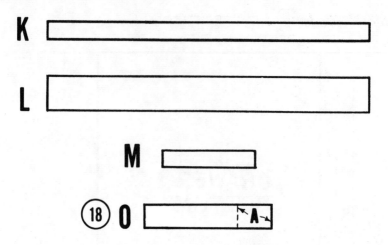

Illus. 14 shows location of K, L. Apply glue to other two K. Nail through L and K to bottom of A using ¾″ brads. This provides a guide for the K fastened to drawer.

Fasten handle M to F with ⅜″ brads. Sandpaper top edge of FGJ and K after assembly. Cut spool holders O from ¼″ dowel. Apply glue and insert in A, in position shown, Illus. 8.

Cut four legs N, Illus. 9, from ⅜″ dowel. Cut ends to angle shown, Illus. 9. Apply glue. Insert legs in A. Drive N through A so it projects slightly above face of A. Sandpaper N flush with A after glue sets.

Countersink heads of all exposed brads. Fill holes with wood filler. Sandpaper surfaces smooth, round sharp edges. Paint or stain following manufacturer's directions on can of finish selected, or leave natural.

CIGARETTE AND MATCH CRADLE

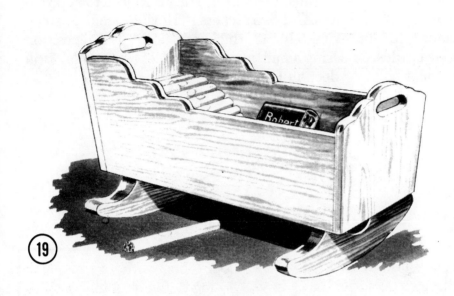

Illus. 19 shows a miniature colonial cradle that makes a popular cigarette and match holder. Illus. 20 shows position of each part.

LIST OF MATERIALS
1 — ¼ x 5 x 36″ surfaced to approximately ³⁄₁₆″ thickness for A, B, C, D
1 — ½ x 2 x 10″ for E
¾ wire brads
4 — ½ x No. 4 screws

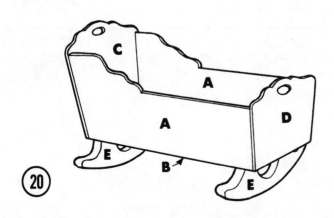

Cut two sides A, Illus. 21; one bottom B, Illus. 22; one head C, Illus. 23; one end D, Illus. 24, from ¼″ stock surfaced to approximately ³⁄₁₆″ thickness. Cut two rockers E, Illus. 25, from ½″ stock planed to approximately ⅜″ thickness. Hold E in position shown, Illus. 22. Using a nail, mark location of screw hole. Drill ¹⁄₁₆ pilot holes ¼″ deep in E, to receive screws.

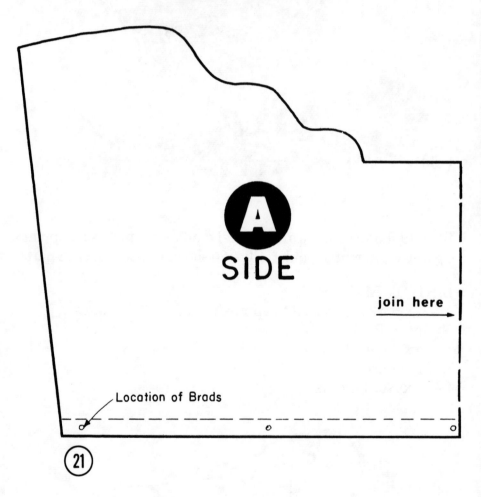

A

SIDE

join here

Location of Brads

㉑

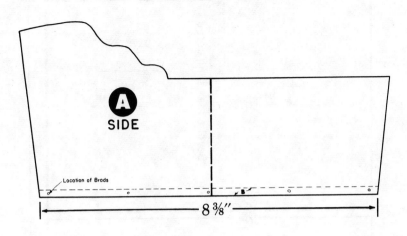

A

SIDE

Location of Brads

B

8 ⅜″

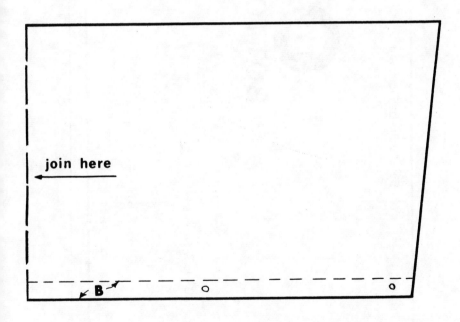

join here

B

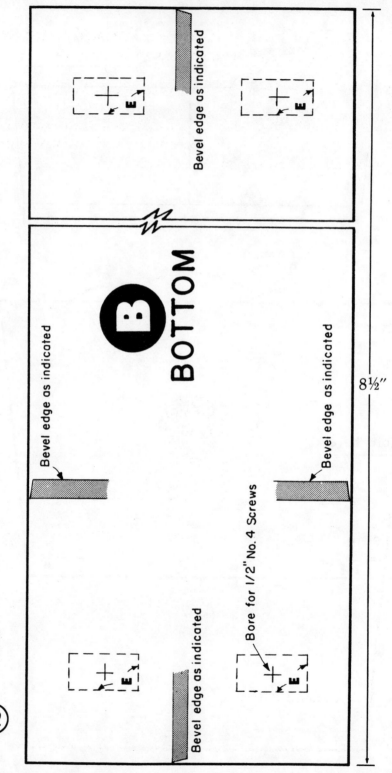

Bore four $\frac{7}{64}''$ holes in B in position indicated to receive #4 screws, Illus. 22. Plane edges of B to angle indicated.

Apply glue and nail A to B; C and D to A and B using $\frac{3}{4}''$ brads.

Glue and screw B to E with $\frac{1}{2}''$ No. 4 brass flathead screws. Set all brads and fill holes with woodfiller. Sand surfaces smooth, round all edges. Paint, stain or leave natural.

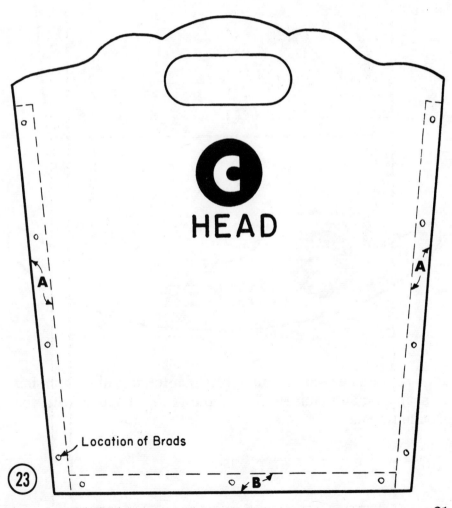

Location of Brads

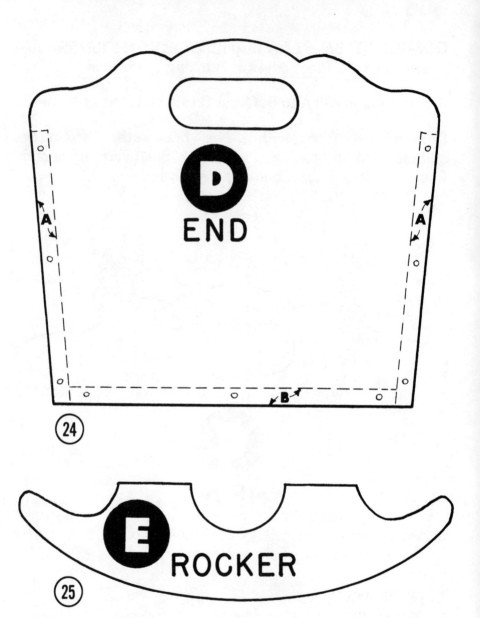

If cradle is to be used as a miniature planter, fold aluminum foil to shape cradle requires. This cradle is very popular with the Dollhouse Set.

COMBINATION PLANT AND STRING HOLDER

(26)

This hanging wall cabinet, Illus. 26, is a popular seller at church bazaar and other fund raising affairs. It's a good starter project for everyone, regardless of age or woodworking ability.

LIST OF MATERIALS
1 — ½ x 6 x 40″ surfaced to approx. ⅜″ thickness
1 pr. ¾ x ¾ hinges
1 wood or metal door pull
1 cabinet door spring catch

Cut one back A, Illus. 27; two B, one D, Illus. 28; and two C, Illus. 29, 30. Bore ³⁄₁₆″ hole in bottom shelf where indicated. Apply glue and nail C to A; C to B and A to B, Illus. 29.

23

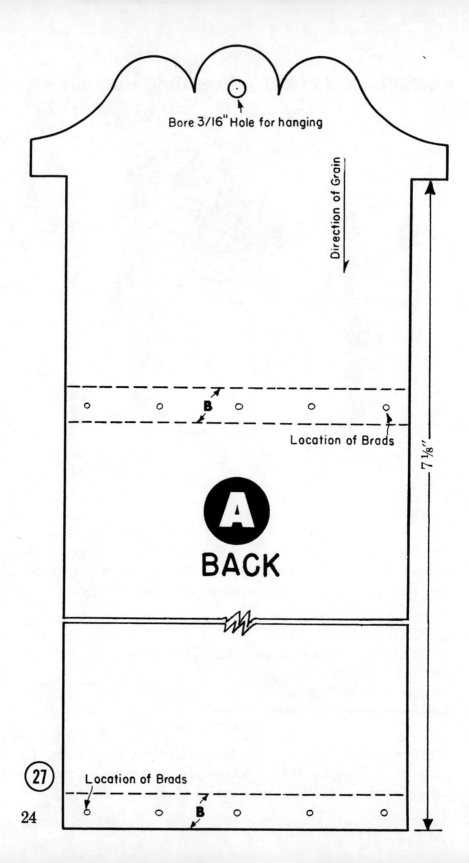

Bore 3/16" Hole for hanging

Direction of Grain

A

BACK

B

Location of Brads

7 1/8"

(27)

Location of Brads

B

24

Recut pattern B along dash line and cut one door D. Bore hole to receive door pull screw where indicated. Notch edge of door thickness required to receive hinges. Fasten door in position with ¾ x ¾ narrow butt hinges with screws provided.

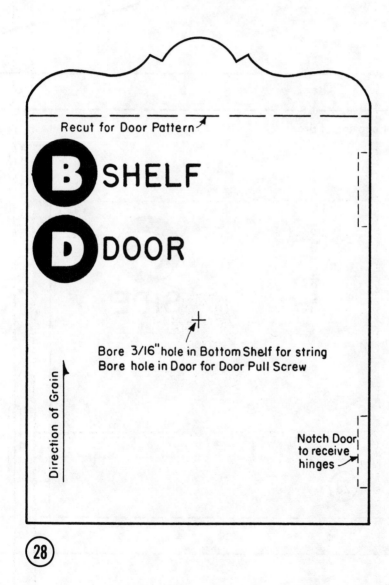

Recut for Door Pattern

B SHELF

D DOOR

Bore 3/16" hole in Bottom Shelf for string
Bore hole in Door for Door Pull Screw

Direction of Grain

Notch Door
to receive
hinges

28

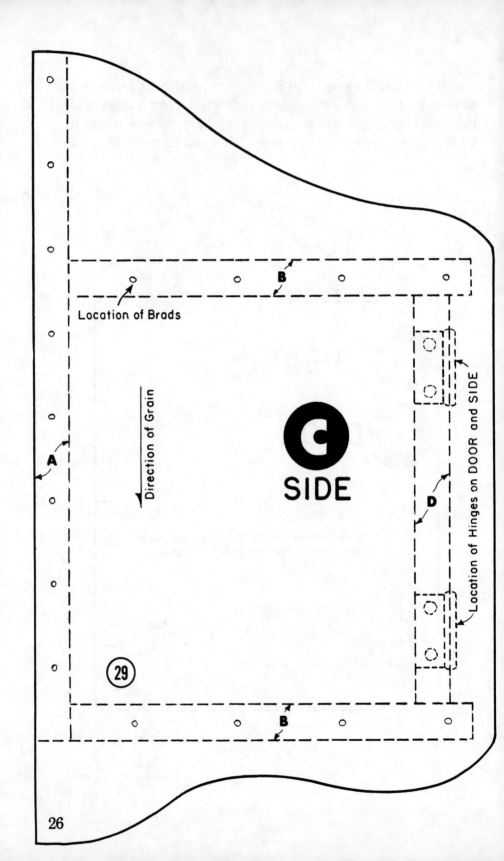

Location of Brads

Direction of Grain

Location of Hinges on DOOR and SIDE

C SIDE

A

B

B

D

㉙

26

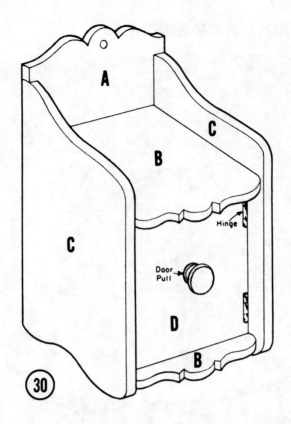

Countersink all screw heads, fill holes with wood filler. Sand all surfaces. Fasten a wood or metal door pull to door. Install cabinet door spring catch following manufacturer's directions. Paint or stain or leave natural.

If you want to use as a plant holder, saw hole in top shelf to size flower pot requires. If you use a shallow pot, you can still put in a small ball of string. Insert end of string through hole in bottom. If you fasten a small cup hook to bottom, you can hang a small pair of scissors.

FERN SCROLL SAW SHELF

The fern scroll saw shelf, Illus. 31, has great appeal. It's a time consuming project that offers hours of complete escape. Drill starting holes where saw blade requires same.

LIST OF MATERIALS
1 – ¼ x 11 x 15″ plywood – A
1 – ½ x 8 x 9″ – shelves

You can make this project using ¼ prefinished hardwood plywood, or ¼, ⅜ or ½″ pine, maple or other hardwood. Use ⅜ or ½″ wood for shelves.

28

If you have a scroll saw capable of cutting through two thicknesses of wood selected, brad the two pieces together. Trace the pattern on the top piece. To simplify getting started, drill several ⅛″ holes in line or a ¼″ hole in each opening.

Pattern A is in three pieces. Join where indicated, Illus. 32. Cut two sides to shape of full size pattern, Illus. 33. Miter inside edge to 45° as noted, Illus. 33 A. Apply glue and nail sides together, Illus. 31, using 1″ brads.

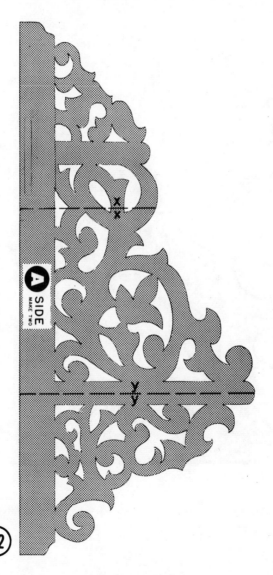

A SIDE MAKE TWO

32

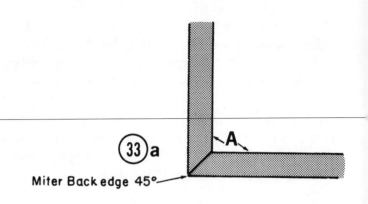

(33) a

Miter Back edge 45°

join here

(33)

join here

X join here

join here

A SIDE
MAKE TWO

join here

A

33

Cut bottom shelf B, Illus. 34, to full size of pattern. Pattern is in two sections. Join where indicated. Recut pattern along dash lines and cut top shelf C. Apply glue and nail A to B and C with 1″ brads. Sandpaper and finish as previously described.

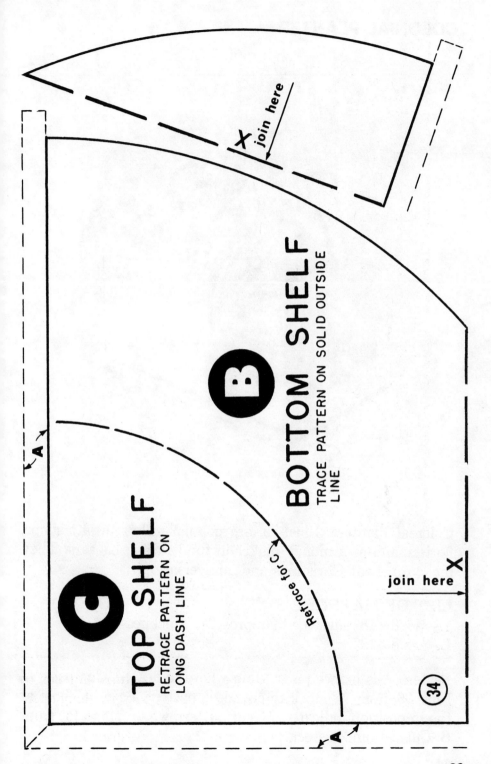

C

TOP SHELF

RETRACE PATTERN ON
LONG DASH LINE

B

BOTTOM SHELF

TRACE PATTERN ON SOLID OUTSIDE
LINE

Retrace for C

A

A

join here X

X join here

34

COLONIAL PLANTER

Colonial Planters, Illus. 35, are popular sellers in gift shops, florists, and as a money maker in fund raising bazaars. They make excellent Christmas and anniversary gifts.

LIST OF MATERIALS
1 – ¼ x 8 x 18″ surfaced to approx. ³⁄₁₆″ thickness – A, B, C
1 – ½ x 8 x 12″   ″   ″   ″   ³⁄₈″   ″   – D

Pattern A is in two parts. Join where indicated. Cut back A, Illus. 36, from ¼″ stock to shape of pattern. Bore ³⁄₁₆″ hole at top in position indicated. Recut pattern where noted for front B. Cut B from ¼″ stock.

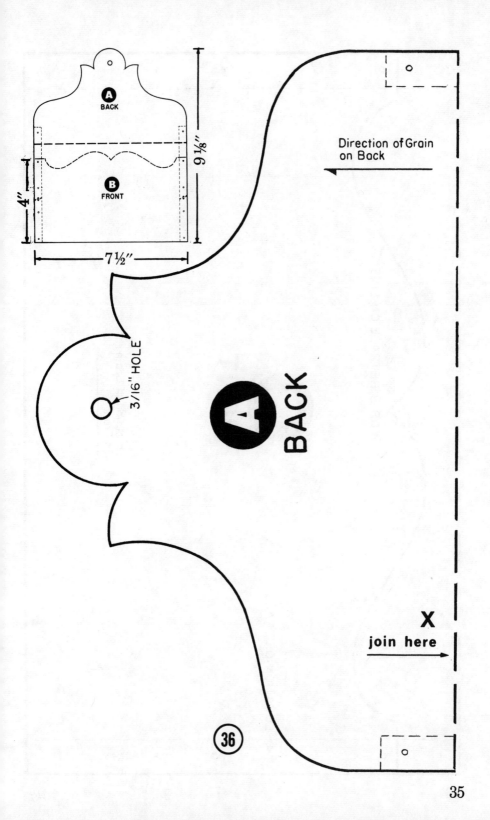

A BACK

BACK

A BACK

B FRONT

9 1/8"

4"

7 1/2"

Direction of Grain on Back

3/16" HOLE

X

join here

36

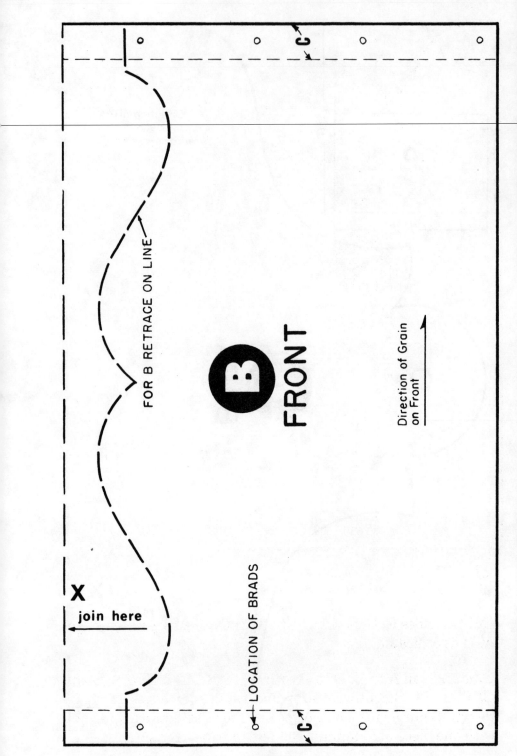

FOR B RETRACE ON LINE

B
FRONT

Direction of Grain
on Front

X
join here

LOCATION OF BRADS

C

C

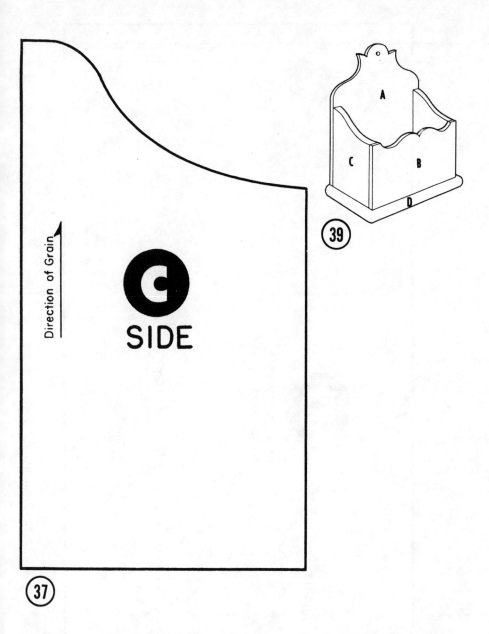

Cut two sides C, Illus. 37; one bottom D, Illus. 38. Shape edges of D as indicated.

Glue and nail A to C; B to C with ¾″ brads. Nail D to A, B and C, Illus. 39. Smooth surfaces and sandpaper edges to shape shown. Countersink nail heads and finish as desired. Line box with one piece of aluminum foil folded to act as a liner.

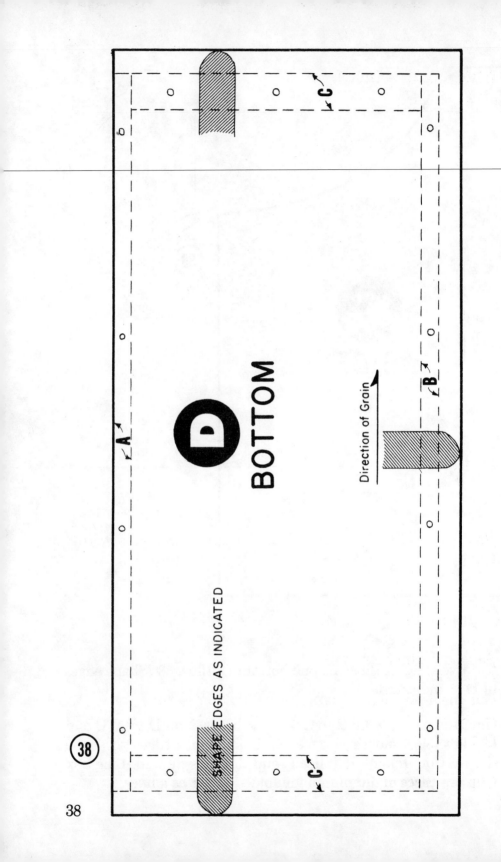

SHAPE EDGES AS INDICATED

D

BOTTOM

Direction of Grain

A

B

C

38

PONY BOOK ENDS

(40)

Illus. 40 shows an easy to make pair of attractive bookends that add much to a child's room.

LIST OF MATERIALS
1 — 1 x 6 x 30"
1 doz. — 1¼" No. 8 flathead wood screws
Scrap of leather for ears

Cut one head. Illus. 41 provides a full size pattern.

Cut one body, Illus. 42.

Cut two bases and two ends, Illus. 43, to size of pattern.

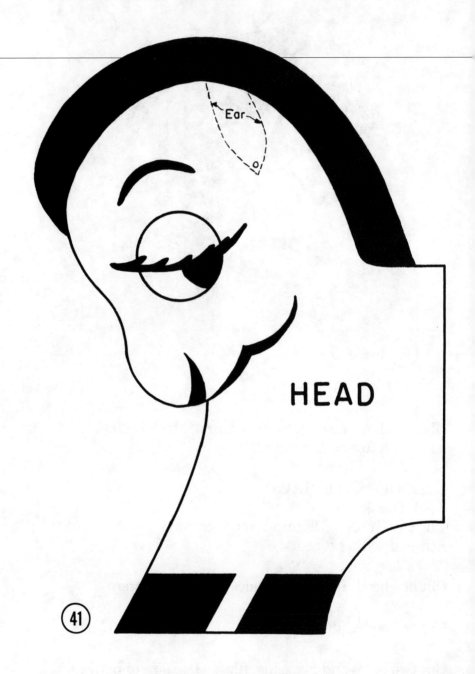

Ear

HEAD

41

COLOR SCHEME

TAN – Head, Body and Eyelid
BLACK – Hoofs, Eyebrow, Eyelash, Mane, Tail,
Pupil and outline of Eye and Chin
RED – Mouth, Base and Ends
WHITE – Eyeball and highlights on Hoofs

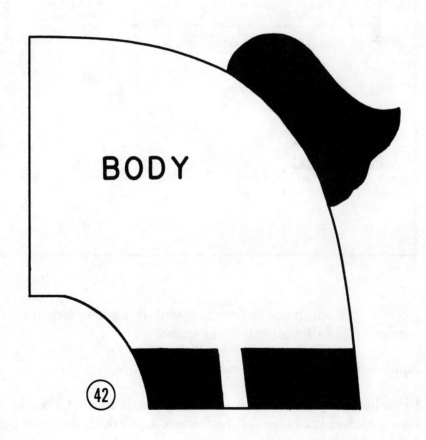

BODY

42

41

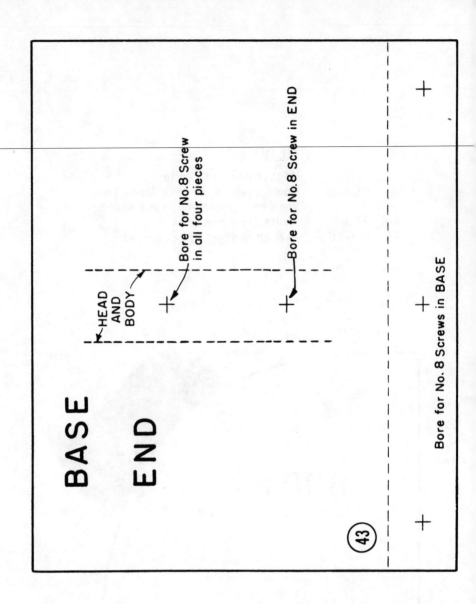

Bore $^{11}\!/_{64}''$ shank holes in base and end in position indicated to receive $1\frac{1}{4}''$ No. 8 flathead wood screws.

Apply glue and screw base to end.

Place head in position between dash lines, Illus. 43. Check location and drill hole through end where needed. Fasten end and base to head; fasten base and end to body, Illus. 44.

42

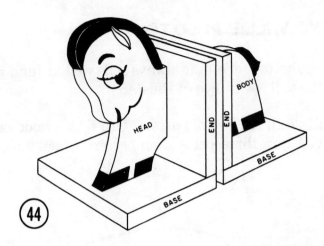

(44)

Finish by sandpapering as previously described. Paint entire project with coat of white primer. When dry replace pattern and trace decorating outlines.

Paint colors in position color scheme suggests.

When dry, cut ears from scrap leather and fold to shape shown on full size pattern, Illus. 45. Nail in position to head, Illus. 41.

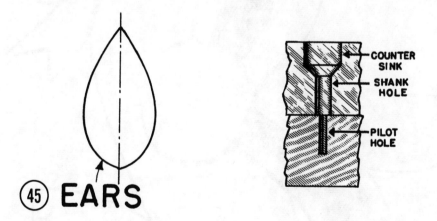

(45) **EARS**

To keep book ends from sliding on a glass surface, glue felt to base.

WADDLING WILLIE PULL TOY

Another popular toy, one that always sells well at fund raising bazaars is the pull toy shown in Illus. 46.

Cut A, Illus. 47, to full size of pattern. Use ¾″ plywood or lumber. Pattern A is in three parts. Join pattern where indicated.

A

join here

join here

X

Y

(47)

46

A

LIST OF MATERIALS
1 — ¾ x 9 x 9″ — A
1 — 1 x 4 x 18″ — B, C, D, E
1 — ¼ dowel 2¾″ — F
2 — 1½″ No. 8 flathead screws
2 — 1¼″ No. 8   ″   ″
2 — 1½″ No. 8 roundhead screws
1 — ⅜″ screw eye

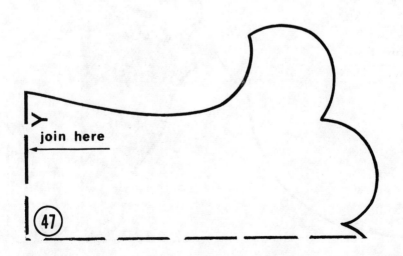

Y

join here

47

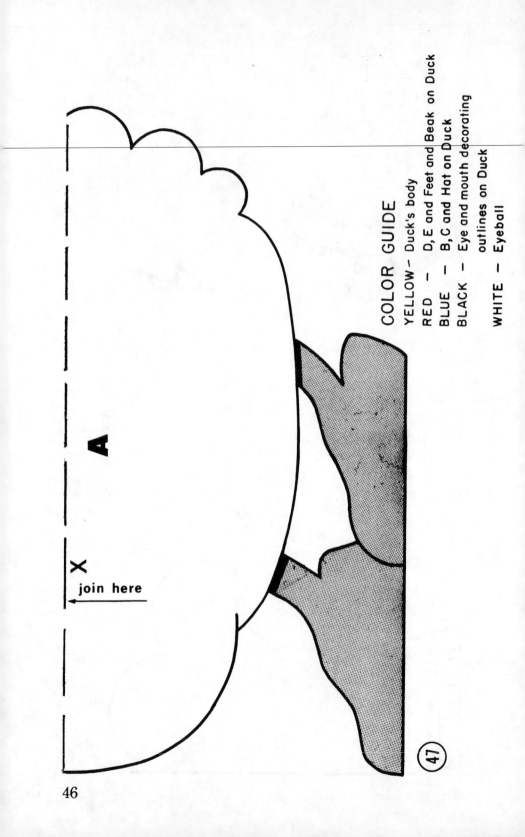

join here

X

A

COLOR GUIDE

YELLOW – Duck's body

RED – D, E and Feet and Beak on Duck

BLUE – B, C and Hat on Duck

BLACK – Eye and mouth decorating
outlines on Duck

WHITE – Eyeball

(47)

46

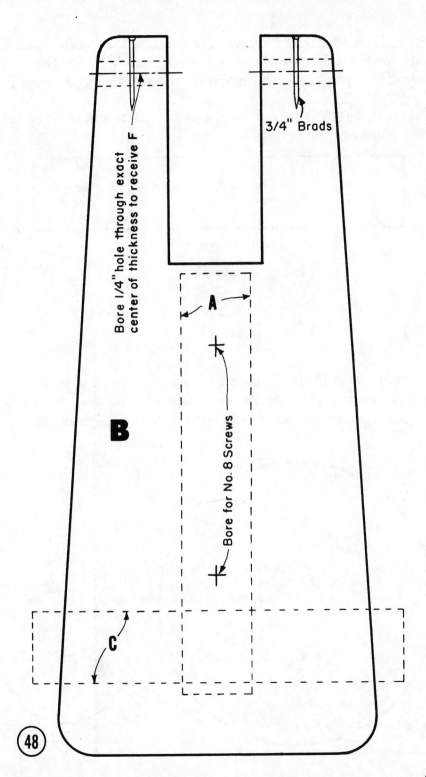

3/4" Brads

Bore 1/4" hole through exact center of thickness to receive F

A

B

Bore for No. 8 Screws

C

48

47

Cut B, Illus. 48, from ¾″ plywood or from 1 x 4. Bore ¹¹⁄₆₄″ shank holes for No. 8 screws where indicated. Bore ¼″ holes through edge of B in position dash lines indicate to receive axle dowel F.

Cut one C to size shown, Illus. 49. Bore ¹¹⁄₆₄″ shank holes to receive No. 8 screws.

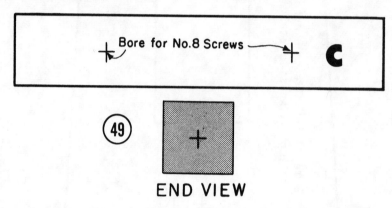

Bore for No.8 Screws — C

(49)

END VIEW

Cut rear wheel D, Illus. 50. Bore hole in position indicated to receive ¼″ dowel. Off center hole activates an up and down movement when pulled. Bore hole so D moves freely on axle F.

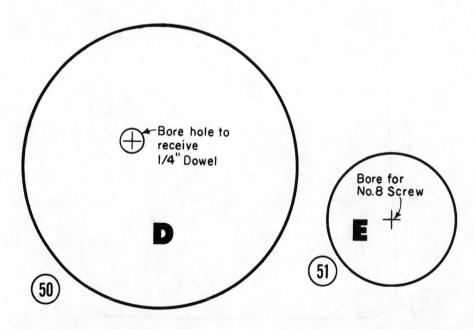

Bore hole to receive 1/4″ Dowel

D

(50)

Bore for No.8 Screw

E

(51)

Cut two front wheels E, Illus. 51. Bore $^{11}\!/_{64}''$ hole so 1½" No. 8 roundhead screw axle allows wheels to move freely.

Cut one axle F, Illus. 52, from ¼" dowel.

Apply glue and screw C to B in position shown, Illus. 48, with 1¼" No. 8 screws.

Place wheel D in position, Illus. 53, and drive axle F through B and D. Fasten F in place with two ¾ brads where indicated.

Bore $^5\!/_{64}$ pilot holes in position shown in end of C, Illus. 49. Fasten wheel E to C with 1½" No. 8 roundhead screws. Do not tighten screws. Wheel must turn freely.

Place A in position on B, Illus. 48. With a nail through B, mark A. Drill $^5\!/_{64}$ pilot holes in A to receive No. 8 screws. Apply glue and fasten B to A with 1¼" No. 8 screws.

Sandpaper all surfaces and edges smooth. Paint entire project with a primer. When dry, trace decorating outlines. Paint colors shown in color guide, Illus. 47. Fasten a ⅜" screw eye to front. Tie a pull cord to screw eye.

EASY-TO-BUILD WREN HOUSE

(54)

A wren house, Illus. 54, like the birdhouses offered in Book #669, is a popular build-it item for every age.

LIST OF MATERIALS
1 — ½ x 6 x 40″ exterior grade plywood
    for A, B, C, D, E, F
1 — ⅜″ dowel for G
2 — ½″ screw eyes

Cut one front and back to full size and shape of pattern A, Illus. 55. Bore ⅜″ vent holes at top, in both front and back. Bore 1″ entry hole and ⅜″ hole for perch in front only.

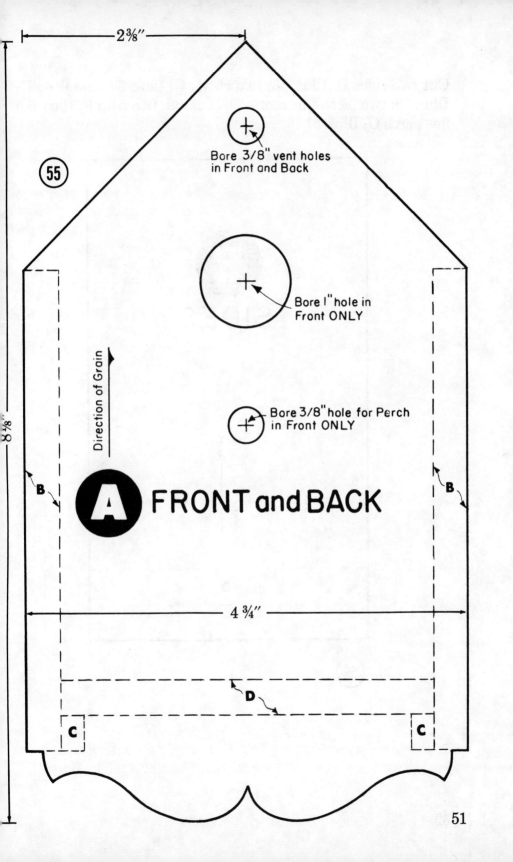

2⅜″

55

Bore 3/8″ vent holes
in Front and Back

Bore 1″ hole in
Front ONLY

Direction of Grain

Bore 3/8″ hole for Perch
in Front ONLY

B

A FRONT and BACK

B

8⅛″

4¾″

D

C

C

51

Cut two sides B, Illus. 56; two cleats C, Illus. 57; one floor D, Illus. 58; two pieces for roof — E, Illus. 59; two trim F, Illus. 60; one perch G, Illus. 61.

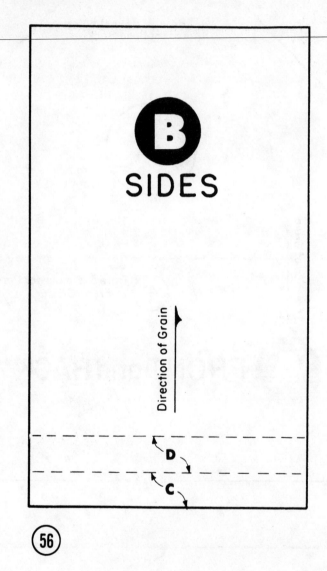

B

SIDES

Direction of Grain

D

C

56

C CLEAT

57

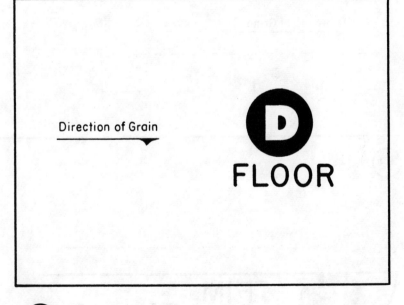

Direction of Grain

D FLOOR

58

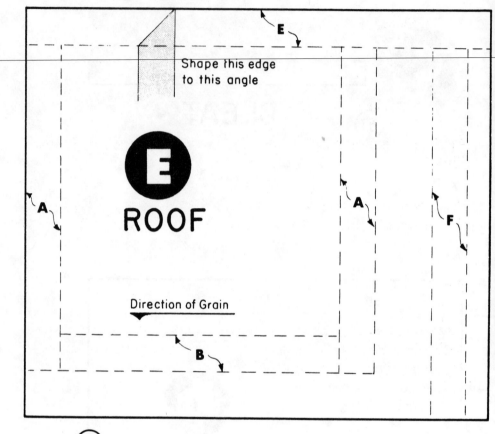

Shape this edge
to this angle

E

ROOF

Direction of Grain

A

B

E

A

F

(59)

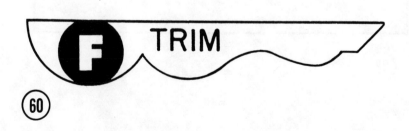

F TRIM

(60)

54

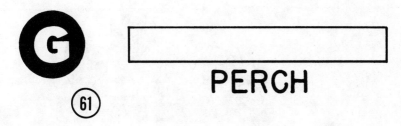

PERCH

Apply glue and nail A to B with 1″ brads; C to B with ½″ brads, Illus. 55.

Plane edge of E to shape shown, Illus. 59. Glue and nail E to A; F to E with 1″ brads, Illus. 54. Drive brads at an angle so they don't protrude.

Cut ⅜″ dowel for G. Apply glue and insert G in A.

To permit cleaning house, floor D isn't nailed. It rests on cleats C, Illus. 55. Paint entire project with exterior paint. Fasten two ½″ screw eyes to roof, Illus. 54. Hang birdhouse from branch with wire.

MARY AND LAMB WALL PLAQUE

LIST OF MATERIALS
1 — ¼ x 13¼ x 25″ plywood or hardboard

This scroll saw wall plaque, Illus. 62, makes a very attractive nursery wall decoration. It's an ideal gift for those getting ready for a new arrival. The design can also be traced on the wall and repeated, end to end. The full size pattern, Illus. 63, is in five parts, Illus. 64, 65, 66, 67, 68. Join in position shown, Illus. 63.

Connect parts at X, Y, Z, also at bonnet. The pattern is joined along dotted lines as well as on long dash lines. Trace outline on plywood, then saw along outside line.

Paint plaque with primer. When dry, trace decorating guides in exact position pattern indicates. If you slip a carbon paper under as you trace, it will give you sharp painting guides.

Noting colors in Color Guide, paint solid areas first. When these have dried thoroughly, paint in eyes, nose, mouth, cheeks, Illus. 63. Paint in black trim, outline of arm, etc., last.

B — BLUE
G — GREEN
P — PEACH
R — RED
W — WHITE
Y — YELLOW
Blk — BLACK

Blk — eyes, nose

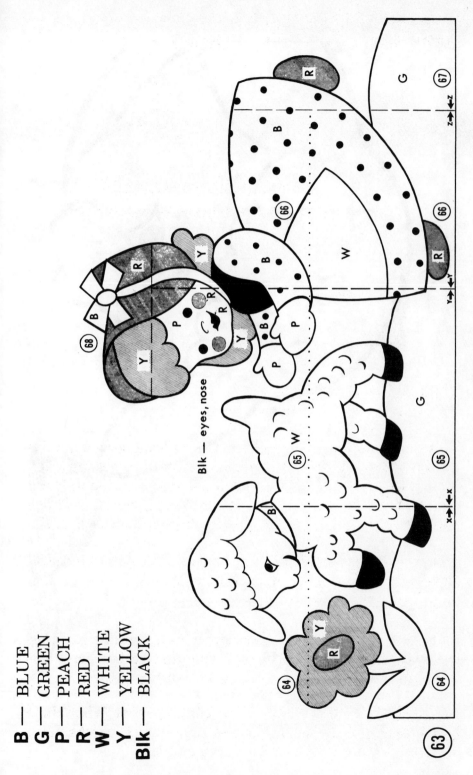

BLUE

64

join here **X**

YELLOW

RED

64

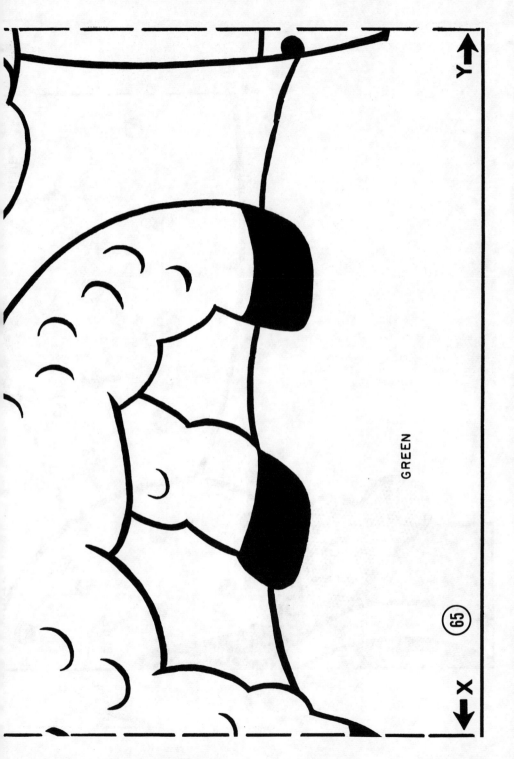

GREEN

Y

X

65

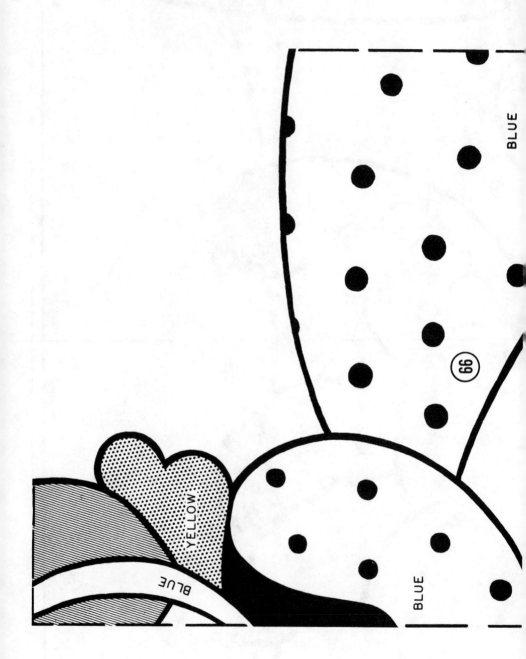

BLUE

YELLOW

BLUE

BLUE

BLUE

99

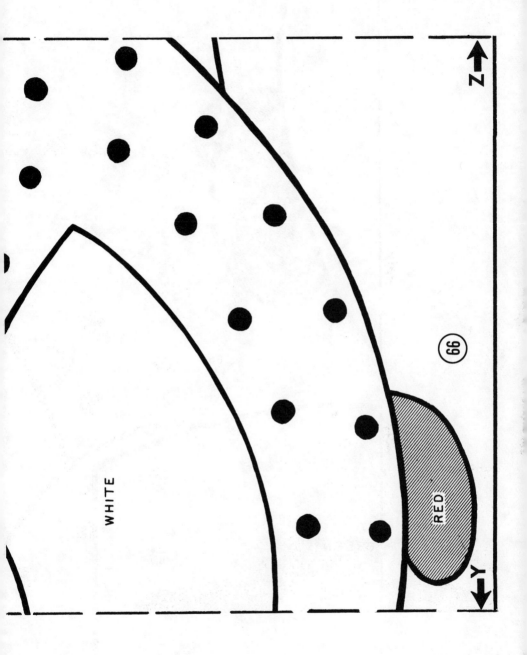

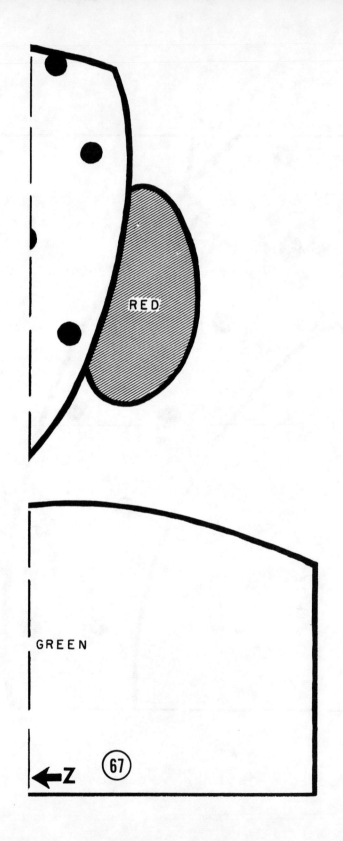

RED

GREEN

←Z (67)

64

Paint in colors in this sequence:

WHITE — Apron, lamb
PEACH — Face, hands
RED — Bonnet, cheeks, shoes, flower center
YELLOW — Hair, flower
BLUE — Skirt ribbon on bonnet and lamb
GREEN — Grass, stem and leaves of flower
BLACK — Polka dots, bodice, hoofs, outlines, facial features, eye on lamb

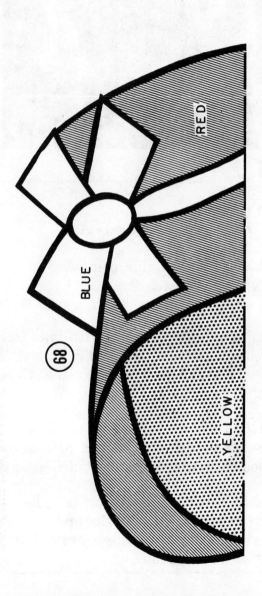

APPLIQUE SHELF

LIST OF MATERIALS

1 — ¼ x 17 x 18″ hardwood or plywood – A, B
1 — ½ x 6 x 36″   ″   ″   ″   – C
⅜″ brads, ten ¾″ No. 6 screws, glue, paint

Solid outside lines indicate pattern. Dash lines show relative position of adjoining part. Pattern A is in 3 parts. Tape at X also at Y. Pattern B is in 2 parts. Connect at Z. Glue all wood-to-wood contacts.

Cut two sides A, two appliques B from ¼″ hardwood or plywood. Cut two shelves C to width indicated on pattern by 18″ long. Use ½″ hardwood or plywood. Round front edge as shown.

Glue and brad B to A with ⅜″ brads. Bore holes for No. 6 screws where indicated on pattern A. Apply glue and screw A to C with ¾″ No. 6 flathead wood screws. Countersink heads of screws and brads. Fill holes with a wood filler.

66

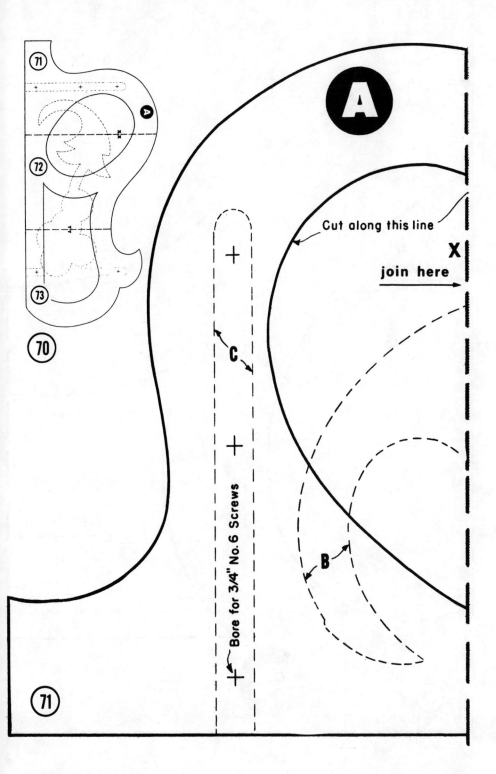

Cut along this line

X

join here

C

B

Bore for 3/4" No. 6 Screws

71

72

73

70

71

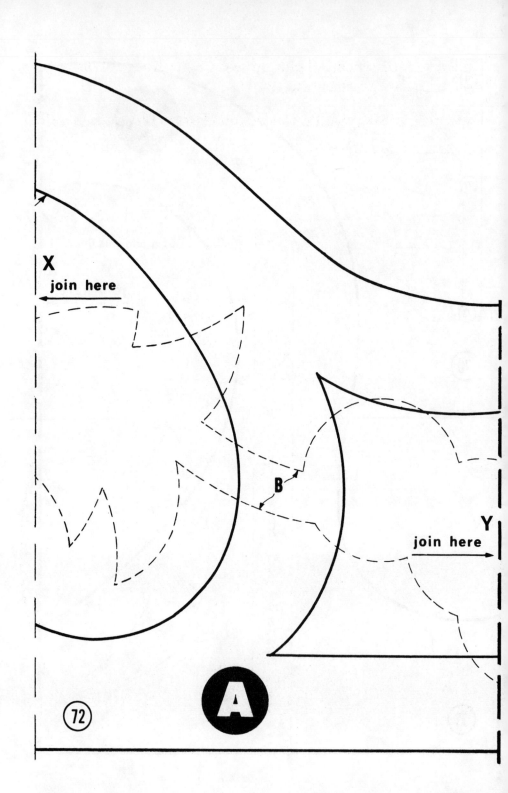

X

join here

B

Y

join here

(72)

A

Sand surfaces smooth. Paint project with a primer. When dry, paint parts with colors suggested.

Hang shelf using two 1½″ angle irons fastened to studs in wall.

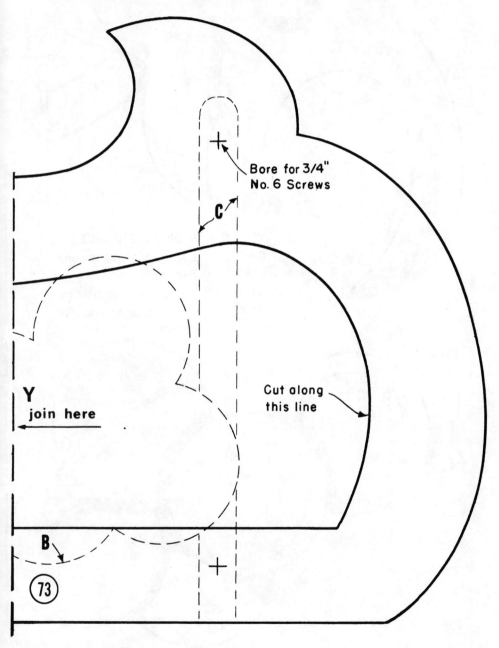

APPLIQUE

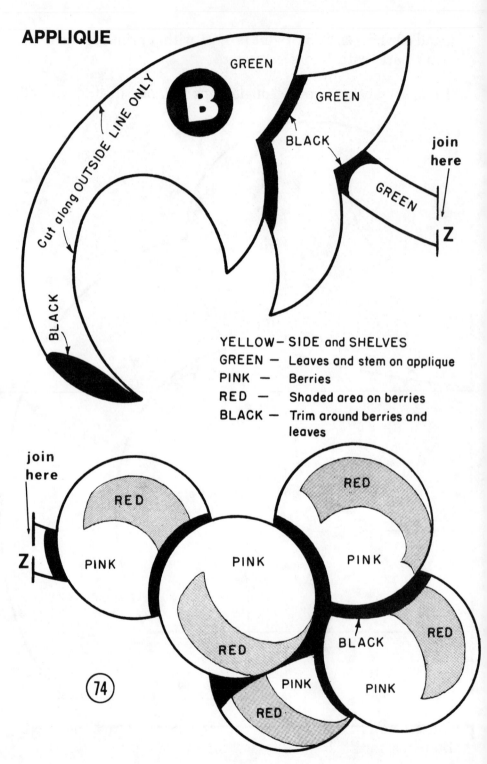

GREEN

GREEN

BLACK

B

join here

GREEN

Z

Cut along OUTSIDE LINE ONLY

BLACK

YELLOW— SIDE and SHELVES
GREEN — Leaves and stem on applique
PINK — Berries
RED — Shaded area on berries
BLACK — Trim around berries and leaves

join here

Z

RED

PINK

PINK

RED

PINK

RED

RED

PINK

BLACK

RED

PINK

(74)

70

LAWN ORNAMENTS

LIST OF MATERIALS

1 — ¾ x 10 x 17″ lumber or exterior grade plywood
1 — ½ x 4½ x 4½″ exterior grade plywood
2 — ⅜ x 8″ iron rods
1 — ¼ x 5″
Paint

COLOR GUIDE
YELLOW – DUCK, CHICK, Beak on Hen
WHITE – HEN, Eyeballs
RED   — Comb and Wattle on Hen, Beaks on Duck and Chick
BLUE   — Feather Outlines on Hen
BLACK — Chick and Duck Feather Outlines, Eyeballs,
          Eye and Mouth Outlines

Solid black outside lines indicate pattern.

The Duck is full size in two parts. The Hen is full size in three parts. Connect Hen at Y and in position outline indicates.

Cut Hen and Duck from ¾″ wood or exterior grade plywood. Bore hole for ⅜″ iron rod in position indicated.

71

Cut Chick from ½″ wood. Bore hole for ¼″ iron rod where indicated.

Smooth edges with a file or sandpaper.

Paint edges as well as both surfaces with a primer.

Use carbon paper to trace outlines. Paint in colors suggested on color chart. Use exterior paint.

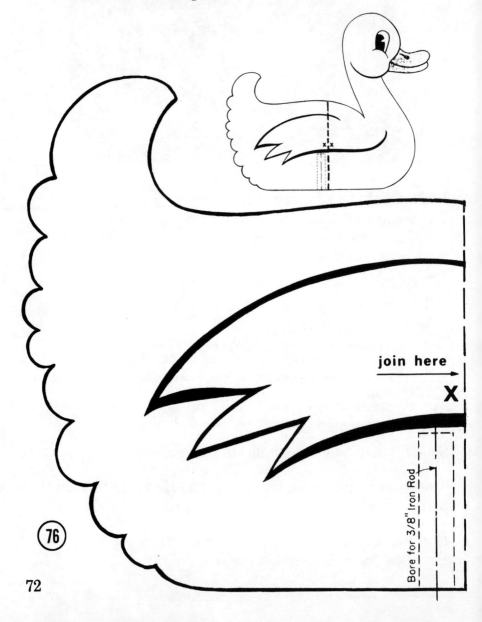

join here ⟶

X

Bore for 3/8″ Iron Rod

⑦⑥

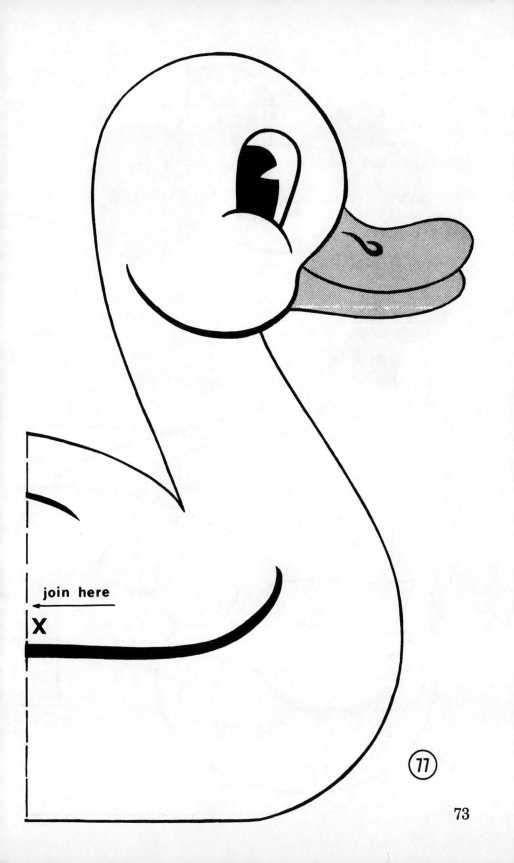

join here

X

⑦⑦

join here →

X

CHICK

Bore for 1/4" Iron Rod

78

79

Insert ⅜ x 8″ rod in Duck and Hen.

Insert ¼ x 5″ rod in Chick. Press rods into ground to stand ornaments on lawn.

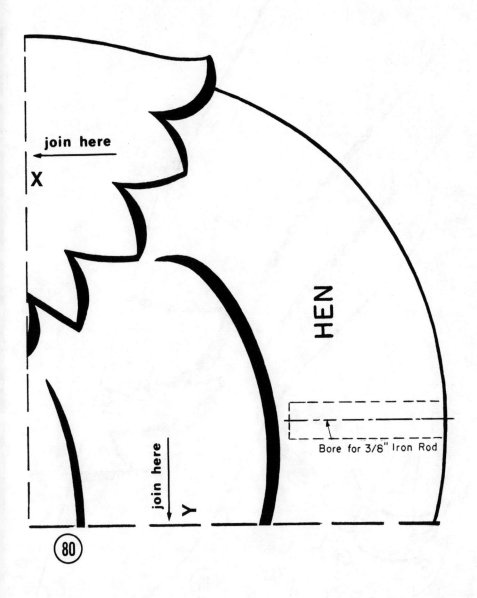

join here

X

HEN

Bore for 3/8″ Iron Rod

join here

Y

80

join
here
Y

79

80

81

HEN

81

LAWN ORNAMENT

LIST OF MATERIALS
1 — ½ or ⅝ x 9½ x 15″ exterior grade plywood
2 — ¼ x 10″ iron rods.

Tape pattern together. Then cut pattern along outside line. Trace and cut shape from ½″ or ⅝″ exterior grade plywood. Paint both sides with exterior primer. Blacken back of pattern with a soft pencil. Attach pattern to cutout with tape. Using a sharp hard pencil trace all decorating guides.

Paint solid areas with color specified in color guide. When dry, paint dark blue polka dots on skirt. Next paint black trim lines on pattern.

Flesh color can be mixed by adding a small amount of red to white paint.

Bore two ¼″ holes, 2″ deep in bottom edge approximately 2″ in from each end. Insert 10″ length of ¼″ iron rod in each hole. Press rods into ground.

COLOR GUIDE

FLESH   – Face, Arms
YELLOW – Hair, Skirt
RED   –   Hair Ribbon, Flower, Flower Pot
DK. BLUE – Polka Dots
GRAY   –   Sprinkling Can
BLACK – Shoes, Trim
GREEN – Grass, Leaves
WHITE – Socks, Blouse, Highlights on
               Shoes

Paint ornament in this sequence:
Face, arms, hair, skirt, hair ribbon,
flower, flower pot, blouse, socks,
shoe highlights, grass, leaves,
sprinkling can, polka dots, eye,
eyebrow, shoes, black outlines
and trim.

FLESH

WHITE

GRAY

(83)

join here

X

78

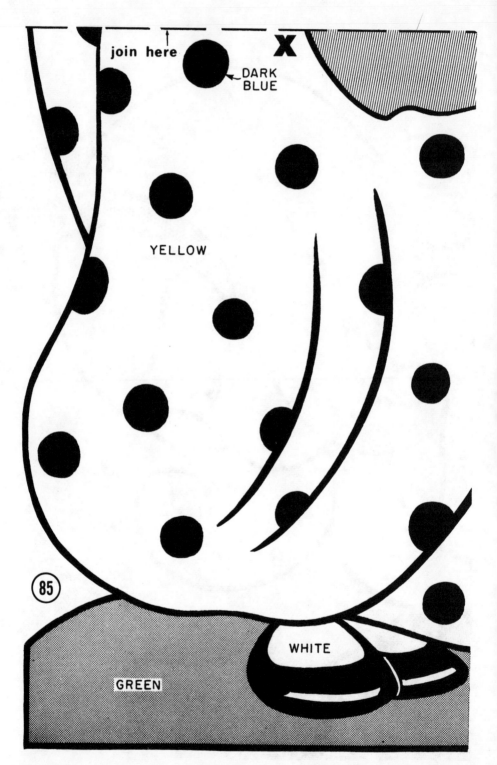

join here

X

DARK
BLUE

YELLOW

⑧⑤

WHITE

GREEN

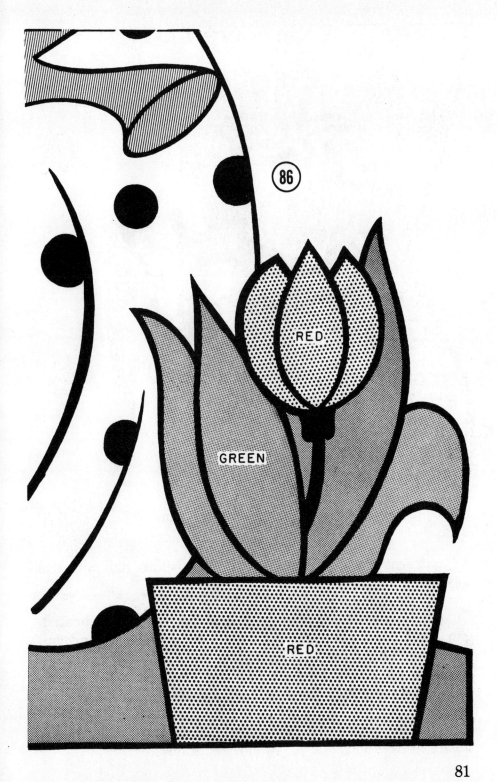

PONY PULL TOY AND PLANTER

(87)

LIST OF MATERIALS
1 — ¼ x 7 x 15″ plywood for A, B, C, D
1 — ⅜ x 6 x 12″   ″   ″ F, G, H
1 — ¾ x ¾ x 5½″ for E
1 — ¼ x 1¼″ dowel
3 — ½″ #6 flathead wood screws
2 — ¾″ #6 flathead   ″   ″
2 — 1″ #8 roundhead wood screws and washers

All patterns are full size. Apply glue before nailing parts together.

Cut one A, two B. Plane edge of A and B to angle indicated. Cut two C. Glue and nail B to A with ¾″ brads. Glue and nail C to A and B. Cut one D from ¼″ plywood. Cut one axle E from 1″ lumber. Notch E to receive D. Cut two wheels F from ⅜″ plywood. Bore hole to receive No. 8 roundhead wood screw.

Fasten D in position to A with three ½″ #6 flathead wood screws. Fasten A to E with two ¾″ #6 flathead screws.

Cut pony G from ⅜″ plywood. Bore hole for ¼″ dowel. Hole must be sufficient size to allow dowel to turn freely.

Cut two wheels H from ⅜″ plywood. Bore hole so ¼″ dowel fits tight in wheel.

Countersink nails. Fill holes with wood filler. Sand surfaces smooth. Round sharp edges with sandpaper. Prime coat all parts using a white primer.

Trace decorating guides on pony. Paint all pieces using colors suggested. When paint has dried, insert washer between end of E and F and fasten F to E with a 1″ #8 roundhead wood screw. Allow wheel F to turn freely on screw.

Cut ¼″ dowel 1¼″. Glue one end to H. Insert dowel through G. Glue other end of dowel to H. Nail D to G with ¾″ brads.

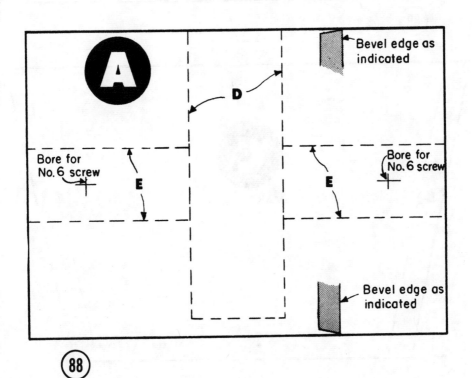

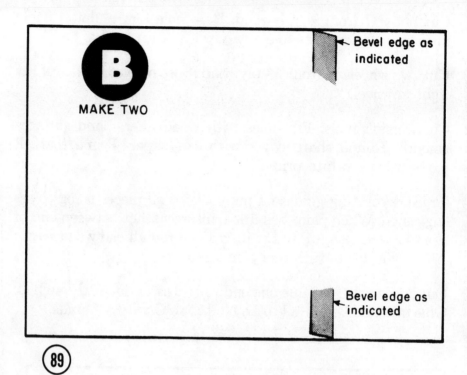

B

MAKE TWO

Bevel edge as indicated

Bevel edge as indicated

(89)

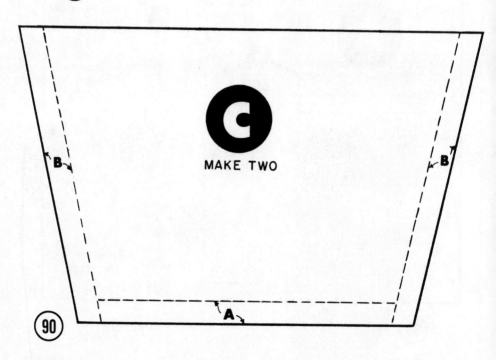

C

MAKE TWO

B

B

A

(90)

84

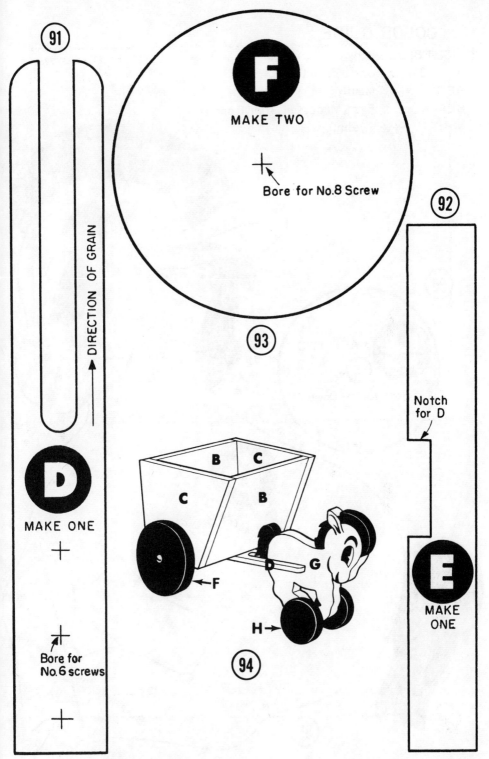

91

F

MAKE TWO

+
← Bore for No.8 Screw

92

DIRECTION OF GRAIN →

D

MAKE ONE

+

+
↗
Bore for
No. 6 screws

+

93

Notch
for D
↘

B   C

C   B

E

MAKE
ONE

D   G

← F

H →

94

85

COLOR GUIDE

LIGHT BLUE – Pony
YELLOW – Cart, E and D
RED   – Mouth
BLACK   – Eyes, Mane, Tail, Trim, F and H
WHITE   – Eyeball

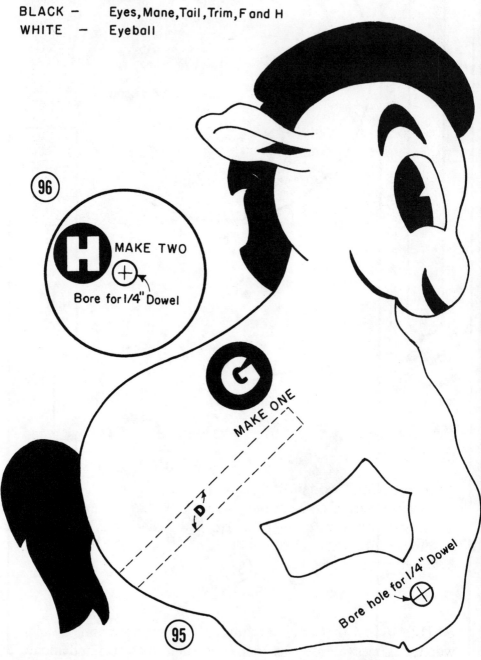

96

H MAKE TWO
Bore for 1/4" Dowel

G
MAKE ONE

D

Bore hole for 1/4" Dowel

95

DOOR STOPS

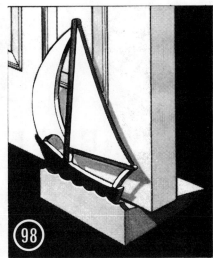

LIST OF MATERIALS
1 — ⅜ x 5 x 7¼″ plywood
1 — 5/4 x 5 x 5″
3 — 1″ #8 flathead screws

RABBIT. Cut pattern along solid outside line. Trace pattern on ⅜″ plywood and saw along outline.

Cut one base from 5/4 x 4½ x 5″. Taper base to shape indicated in End View.

Apply glue and fasten rabbit to base with three 1″ #8 flathead screws in position pattern indicates. Countersink screw heads. Fill holes with a wood filler. Sandpaper project smooth. Apply a primer coat. When dry trace outlines and paint colors in position indicated.

SAILBOAT. Cut out shaded area. Trace pattern on ⅜″ plywood. Follow same step-by-step construction as outlined above.

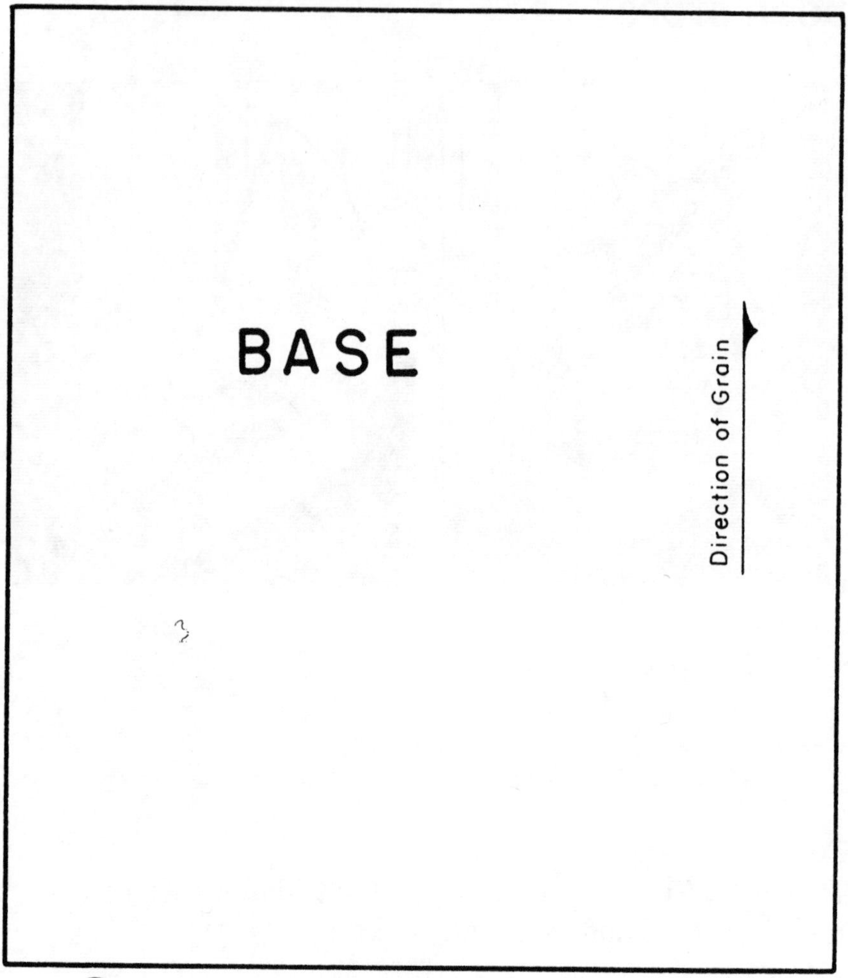

BASE

Direction of Grain

(99)

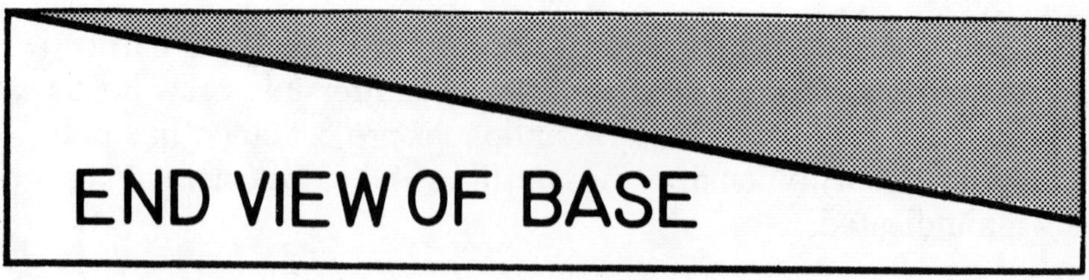

END VIEW OF BASE

(100)

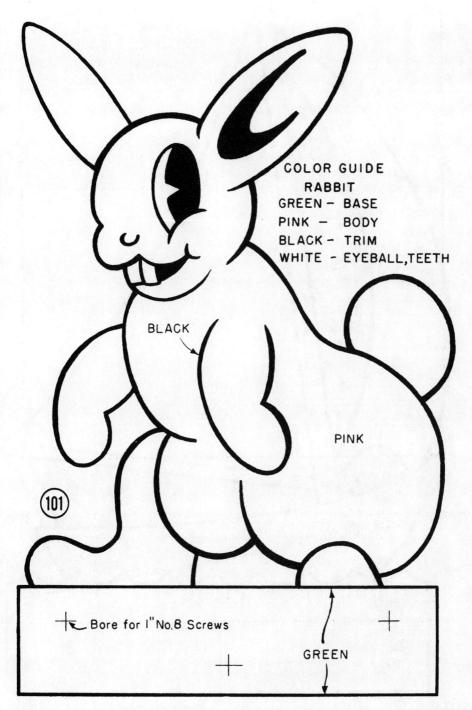

COLOR GUIDE
RABBIT
GREEN — BASE
PINK — BODY
BLACK — TRIM
WHITE — EYEBALL, TEETH

BLACK

PINK

101

Bore for 1" No.8 Screws

GREEN

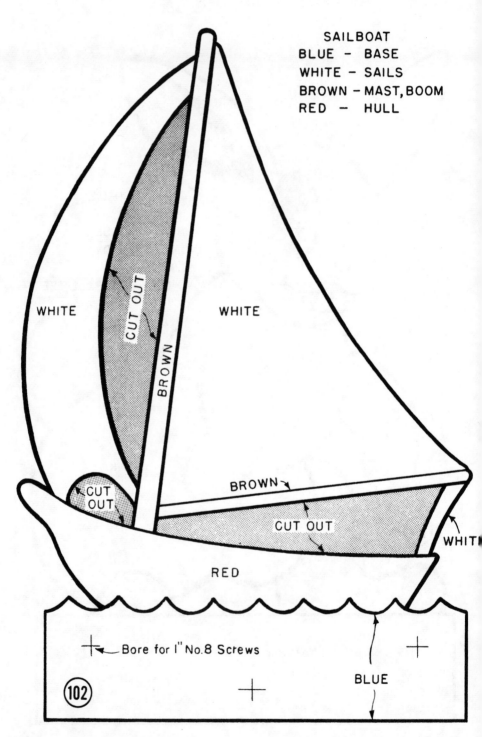

SAILBOAT
BLUE - BASE
WHITE - SAILS
BROWN - MAST, BOOM
RED - HULL

WHITE

CUT OUT

BROWN

WHITE

CUT OUT

BROWN

CUT OUT

WHITE

RED

Bore for 1" No.8 Screws

BLUE

(102)

90

PIERRE THE POTHOLDER'S HOLDER

LIST OF MATERIALS
1 — ⅜ x 10 x 20″ plywood
8 — ¾″ #6 screws
2 — 1½″ #8   ″
2 — 10 penny nails

Solid outside line indicates pattern. Long dash line (— — — —)
indicates where to recut pattern for C.

Short Dash lines (- - - - - - - - -) indicates location of adjoining
parts. Apply glue before fastening parts together. Use ⅜″ plywood for A, B and C.

Cut Chef A. Cut one full circle for B. Bore 7 holes for #6 screws,
two holes for #8 screws in position indicated.

Pattern C is one half. Cut C to full size. Notch C to depth indicated to receive A. Apply glue and fasten B to A with three ¾″
#6 screws; B to C with four ¾″ #6 screws; C to A with one ¾″
#6 screw.

Bore hole in bottom of each leg to receive and hold a 10-penny nail. Bend nails as shown after driving in position. These bent nail "feet" serve as hangers for potholders.

Sand all surfaces and edges smooth. Apply coat of primer. Using carbon paper, trace decorating guides on Chef onto project. Paint A, B and C colors suggested in painting guide. Shelf can be used to hold salt and pepper shakers, spices, a clock, etc.

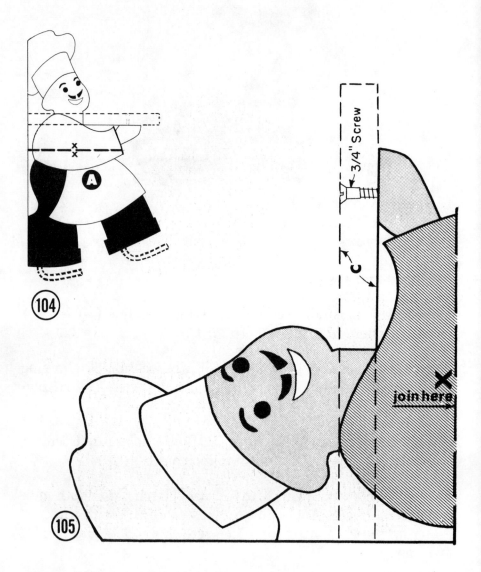

92

COLOR GUIDE

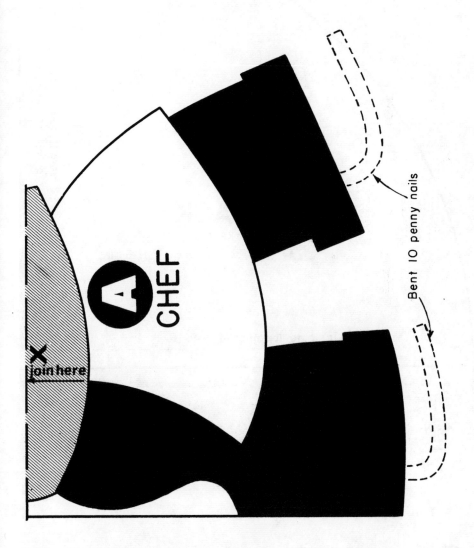

■ BLUE

▨ YELLOW

▦ FLESH

WHITE Apron, Hat, Teeth

BLACK Eyes, Eyebrows, Mustache
    and Outlines

RED Shelf and Back

CHEF

A

X

join here

Bent 10 penny nails

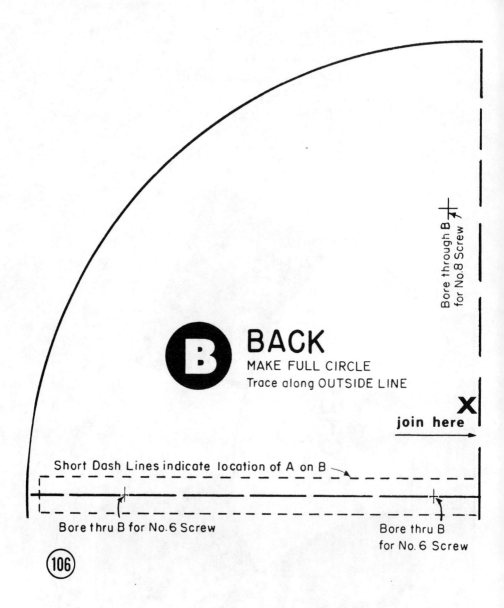

B BACK
MAKE FULL CIRCLE
Trace along OUTSIDE LINE

Bore through B
for No.8 Screw

X
join here

Short Dash Lines indicate location of A on B

Bore thru B for No.6 Screw

Bore thru B
for No. 6 Screw

(106)

94

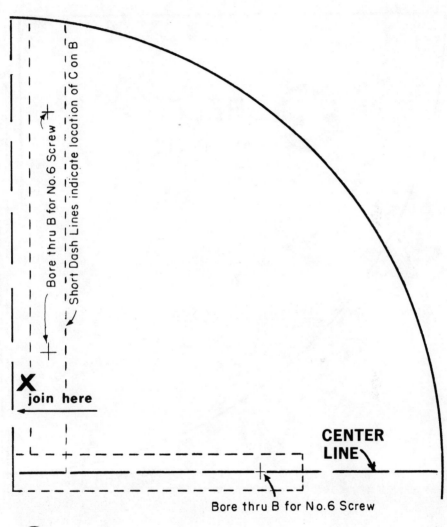

Bore thru B for No.6 Screw

Short Dash Lines indicate location of C on B

X
join here

CENTER LINE

Bore thru B for No. 6 Screw

(107)

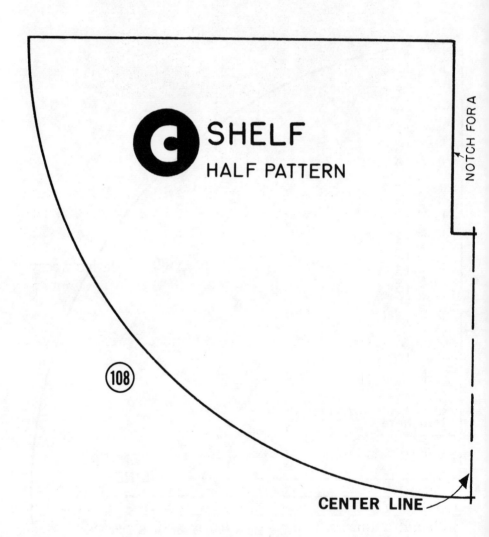

SHELF
HALF PATTERN

NOTCH FOR A

108

CENTER LINE

NAME PLATES

As every homeowner soon learns, identifying one's house with an easy to read name plate and/or house number, helps police and firemen reach it in an emergency.

Making name plate lawn markers, Illus. 109, is relatively easy. The full size alphabet and sign pattern, Illus. 110, simplifies tracing.

If you draw straight lines on a piece of tracing paper, you can trace each letter in position required. Space each letter the exact amount shown on pattern, Illus. 111, 112, 113.

LIST OF MATERIALS
Use 1 x 6 for sign. Use ⅛″ tempered hardboard, ¼ or ⅜″ exterior grade plywood for letters and numbers.

Trace each letter. Drill holes so jigsaw can make cutouts where required. The tracing will indicate overall size of sign. Cut sign to length required. Use pattern for ragged edge, Illus. 110; if you want this kind of a background.

Each letter indicates where to drill shank holes if letters are to be fastened with screws.

A 1 x 2, sharpened at one end, can be used as a stake. Fasten to back of sign with two 1¼″ No. 8 screws.

97

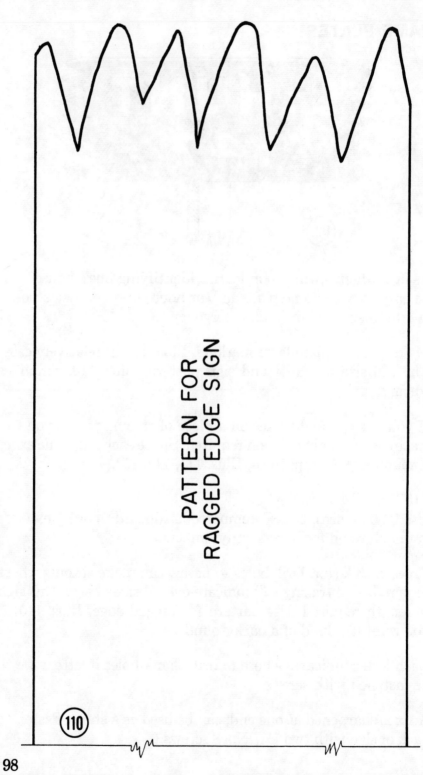

PATTERN FOR
RAGGED EDGE SIGN

(110)

(111)

Paint edges of all letters first. Use exterior grade paint. Don't paint back of letter. Apply exterior glue before fastening each letter or number with screws, nails or escutcheon pins.

INDIAN WALL PLAQUE

Illus. 114 adds a colorful decoration to a child's room. Follow procedure described on page 56. As shown in Illus. 114, the pattern is joined along dotted lines as well as on long dash lines at X, Y and Z. Use ¼″ plywood, ⅛ or ³⁄₁₆″ hardboard. One piece 15 x 25″ will be needed. Paint plaque with following colors.

Paint colors in this sequence:
PEACH — Face, hands
RED — Jacket, moccasins, flower, cheeks, mouth
YELLOW — Pants, center of flower, bow, feather, jacket trim
GREEN — Grass, cactus, feather
BLACK — Hair, eyes, nose, wavy lines on jacket; bear's nose, eye, mouth, cactus points, moccasin stitches, outlines
BROWN — Arrow, bear

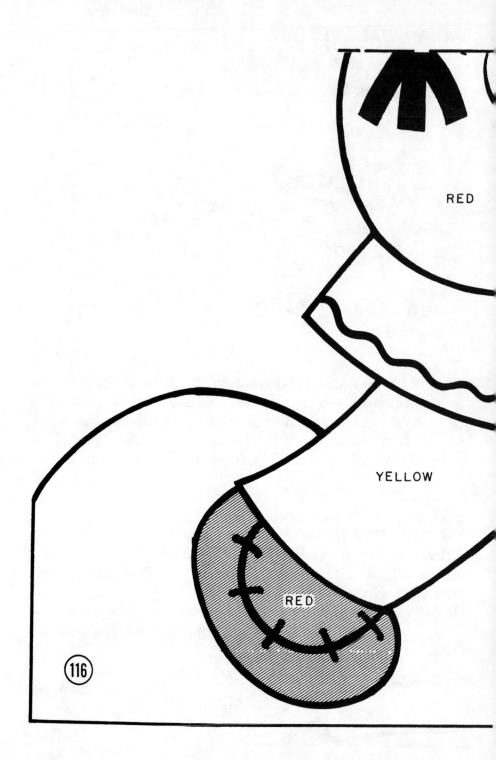

RED

YELLOW

RED

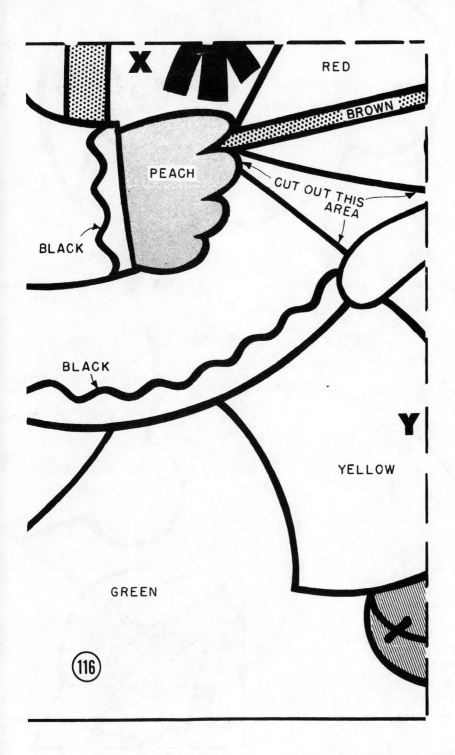

X

RED

BROWN

PEACH

CUT OUT THIS
AREA

BLACK

BLACK

Y

YELLOW

GREEN

116

105

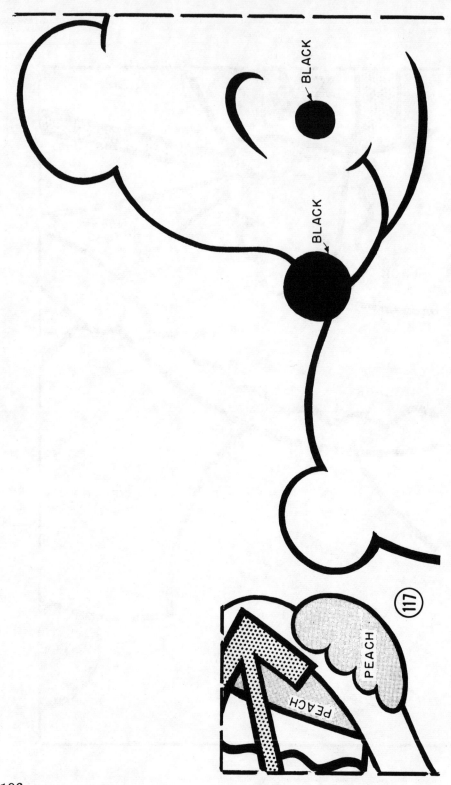

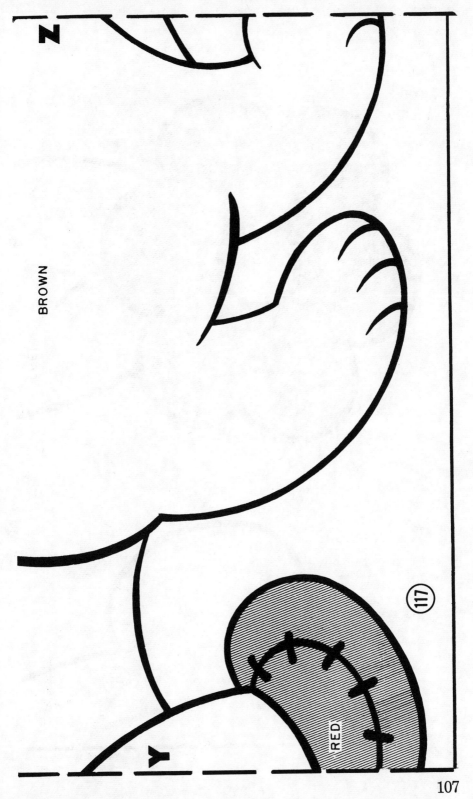

BROWN

N

Y

RED

117

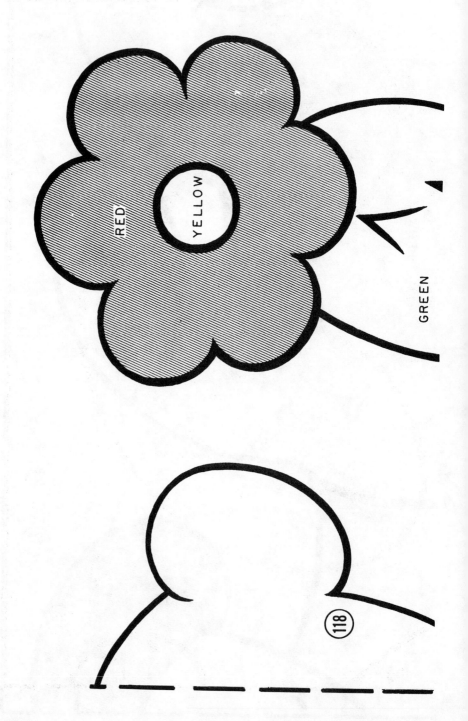

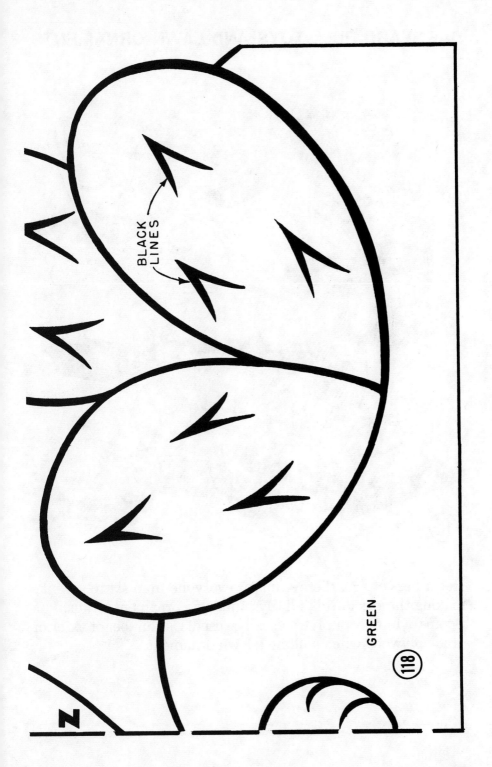

BLACK LINES

N

GREEN

(118)

BARNYARD PULL TOYS AND LAWN ORNAMENTS

(119)

Regardless of age, there's fun for everyone from six to seventy making these colorful pull toys and lawn ornaments, Illus. 119. Scraps of lumber or plywood can be used. Use lumber or exterior grade plywood when making a lawn ornament.

LIST OF MATERIALS
Use plywood
1 — ¾ x 12 x 18″ — A, E, L, O
1 — ½ x 18 x 18″ — B, C, F, M, P, Q, R, S, T, U, X, Y
1 — ⅜ x 3 x 6″ — G, H
1 — ¼ x 6 x 6″ — V, W, Z
12″ — 1⅜″ clothes pole
6″ — 1″ dowel
6″ — ¼″ dowel
Leather scraps — D, J, N
Black coat hanger
8 — 8 penny nails
4 — 6 penny nails
4 — 1″ No. 6 flathead screws
12 — 1½″ No. 7 flathead screws

HOG PULL TOY, Illus. 120. Cut A, Illus. 121, from 1″ lumber or ¾″ plywood. One inch lumber measures ¾″ thick. Cut hind legs B, Illus. 122, and front legs C from ⅜″ plywood. Glue and nail B and C to A in position shown, Illus. 121, using 1″ brads.

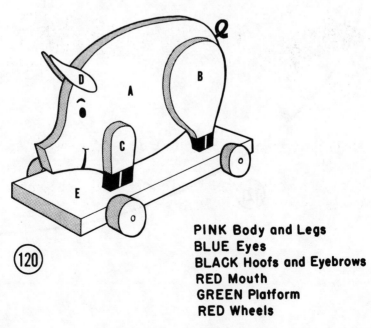

(120)

PINK Body and Legs
BLUE Eyes
BLACK Hoofs and Eyebrows
RED Mouth
GREEN Platform
RED Wheels

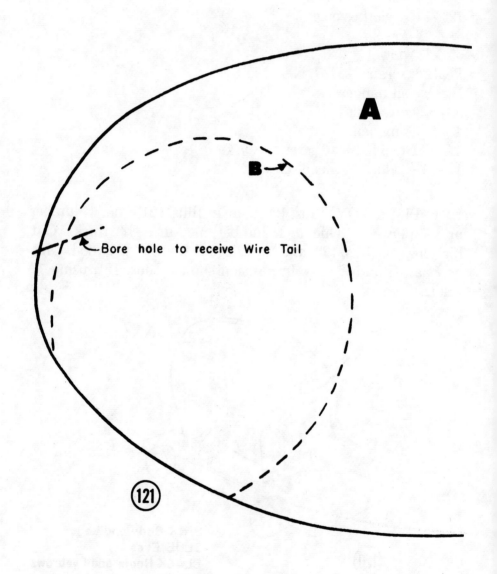

A

B

Bore hole to receive Wire Tail

⑫

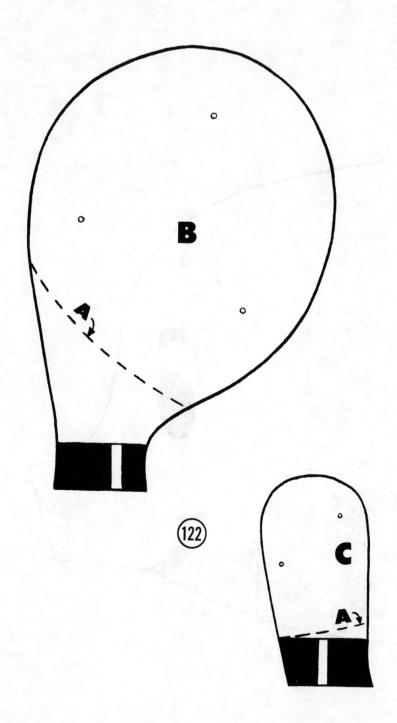

B

A

C

A

(122)

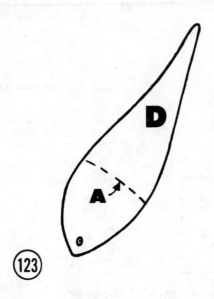

(123)

Cut two ears, Illus. 123, from scrap leather. Tack these in place after all painting has been completed.

Cut base E, Illus. 124, from ¾″ plywood or lumber. Bore pilot holes in edge of E to receive 8 penny common nails for axles. Bore four ⁵⁄₃₂″ shank holes through E, in position noted, to receive No. 7 screws.

Cut four 1″ lengths of 1⅜″ diameter clothes pole for wheels. Drill ⅛″ holes through center so wheels turn freely on 8 penny common nail axles.

Cut a 4″ length of black clothes hanger wire for a hog's tail, Illus. 120. Bend to shape shown. Bore hole to size wire requires.

Glue and screw E to B and C using 1¼″ No. 7 flathead screws.

Attach wheels to E. Apply glue to wire tail and force it into position after hog has been painted. Fasten ears D to A with ½″ escutcheon pins.

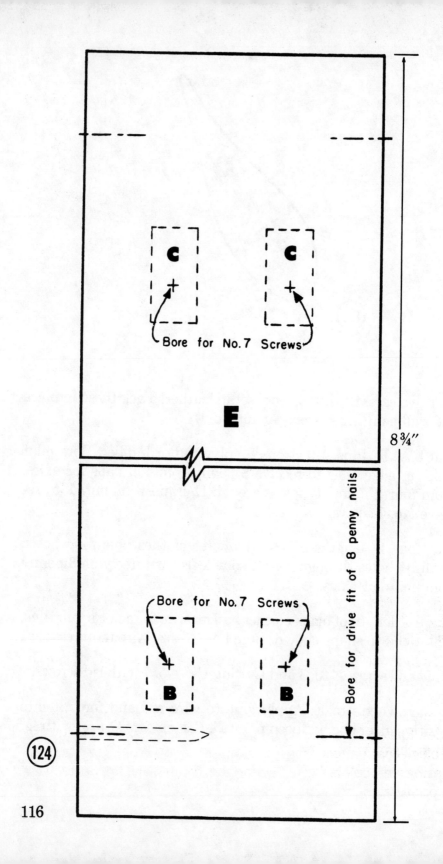

To make a PIG, Illus. 125, use patterns F, G, H, J, K, Illus. 126. Use ½″ plywood for F and K; ⅜″ for G and H. Cut four ¾″ pieces of 1″ dowel for wheels. Use 6 penny common nails for axles.

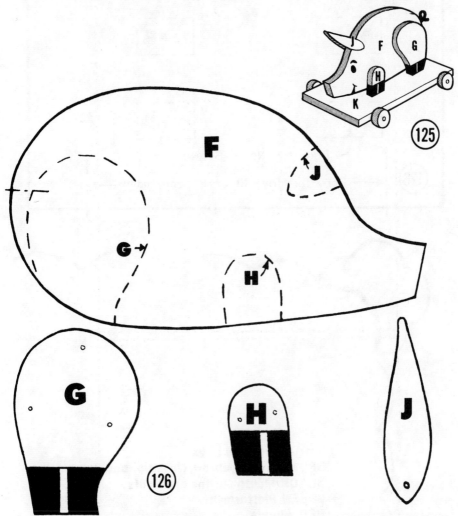

(125)

(126)

Bore four ⁹⁄₆₄″ holes through K in position indicated, Illus. 126, to receive No. 6 screws.

Bore pilot holes through edge of K to receive 6 penny nails for axles. Fasten K to G and H with 1″ No. 6 screws. Cut a 3″ length of black coat hanger. Twist to shape shown, Illus. 125. After decorating with colors suggested for hog, fasten ears, tail and wheels in position.

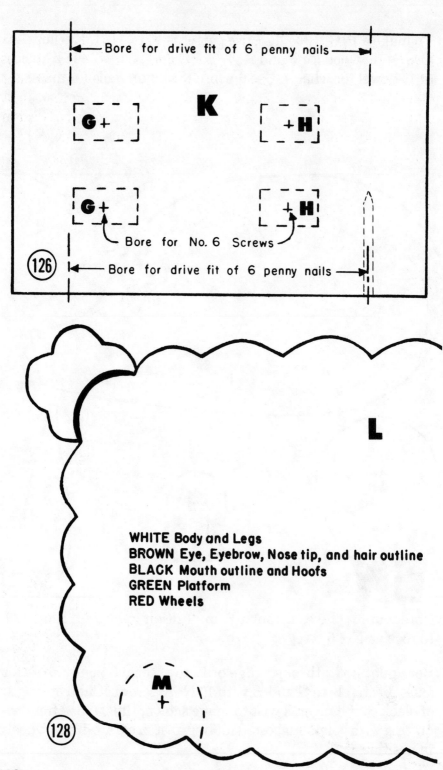

Bore for drive fit of 6 penny nails

G+ **K** **+H**

G+ **+H**

Bore for No. 6 Screws

(126) Bore for drive fit of 6 penny nails

L

WHITE Body and Legs
BROWN Eye, Eyebrow, Nose tip, and hair outline
BLACK Mouth outline and Hoofs
GREEN Platform
RED Wheels

M
+

(128)

The SHEEP, Illus. 127, is cut from patterns L, M, N, O. Pattern L is in two parts, Illus. 128. Legs M and ears N are shown in Illus. 129. The base O is shown, Illus. 130. Follow procedure described for making the hog. Use ¾" plywood or lumber for L and O; ⅜" for legs M. Use brown leather for ears N. Fasten wheels and ears in place after painting in colors suggested.

119

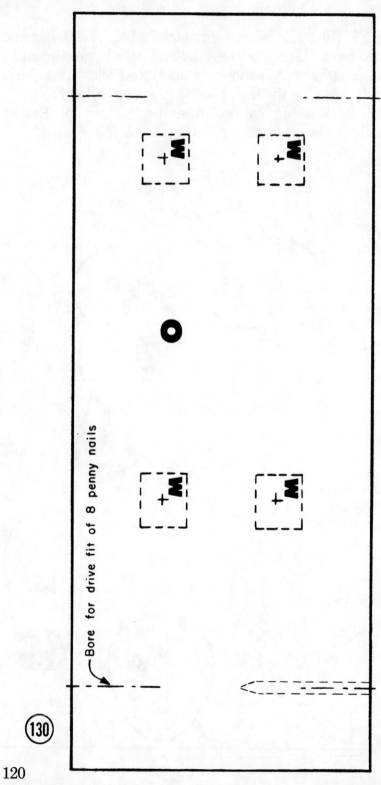

Bore for drive fit of 8 penny nails

The SWAN, Illus. 131, is cut to shape of pattern P, Illus. 132. Cut Q, Illus. 133. Cut P and Q from ⅜″ plywood. Bore two ⁵⁄₃₂″ holes through Q at "q" for two No. 7 screws. Glue and screw Q to P with 1½″ No. 7 screws.

WHITE Body
RED Beak
BLACK Eyebrow and spot on beak
BLUE Eye and wing outline
BLUE Platform

Q

q

s

Bore for 1/4" Dowel

Bore for No. 7 Screws

q

133

R

Q

134

122

The ROOSTER, Illus. 134, is in two parts, join and cut to shape of pattern R, Illus. 135. Use base Q, Illus. 133. Cut both from ½″ plywood.

R

join here

X

Bore for
1/4″ Dowel

R

X X

(135)

Cut ¼″ dowel 1¾″. Bore hole through Q, at "s", to receive dowel. Bore ¼″ hole ¾″ deep in R for dowel. Apply glue to fasten rooster in position. Paint rooster colors suggested.

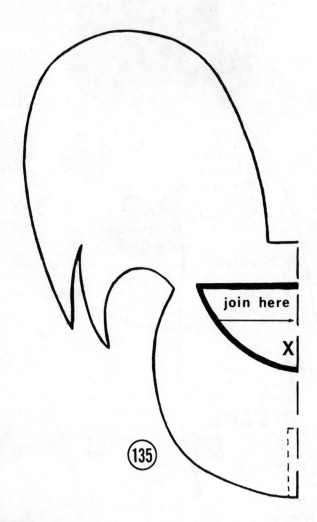

join here

X

(135)

WHITE Body
RED Comb and Wattle
YELLOW Beak, Dowel
BLACK Eyeball, Brow and
        outline of eye.
BLUE feather outline

The DUCK, Illus. 136, is cut to shape of pattern T, Illus. 137. Cut U to size shown, Illus. 138. Cut both from ½″ plywood. Bore ⁵⁄₃₂″ holes at "u" and fasten U to T with No. 7 screws.

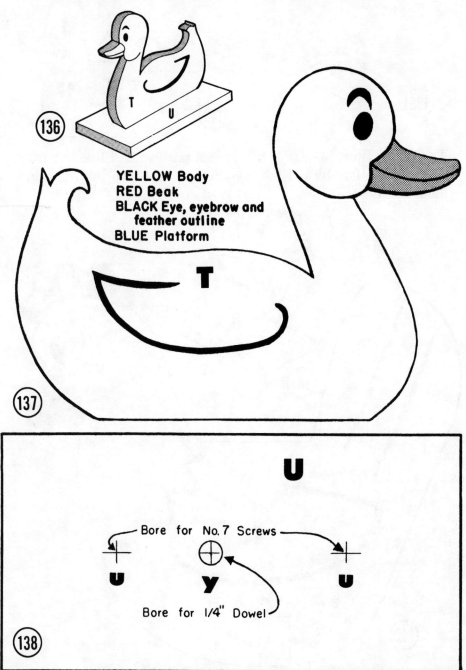

YELLOW Body
RED Beak
BLACK Eye, eyebrow and
    feather outline
BLUE Platform

T

U

Bore for No. 7 Screws

U   y   U

Bore for 1/4" Dowel

The DUCKLING, Illus. 139, is cut to shape of pattern V from ¼″ plywood, Illus. 140. Glue and nail W, Illus. 145, to V with 1″ brads. Paint duckling same colors as duck.

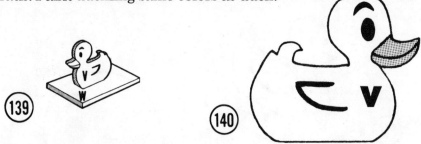

The HEN, Illus. 141, is cut to shape of pattern X, Illus. 142, from ½″ plywood. Use base, Illus. 138. Follow same procedure as outlined for rooster.

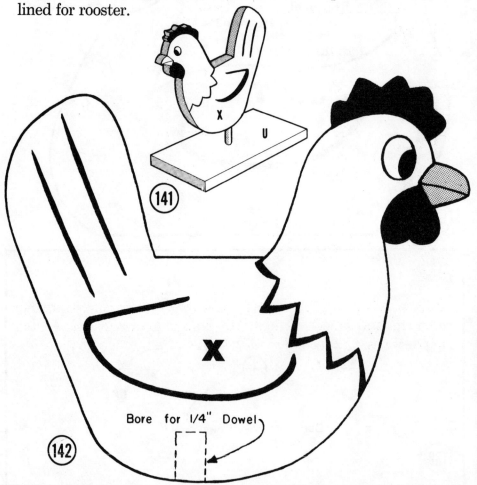

Bore for 1/4″ Dowel

The CHICK, Illus. 143, is cut to shape of pattern Z, Illus. 144, from ¼" plywood. Cut W, Illus. 145, from ¼" plywood. Glue and nail W to Z with 1" brads.

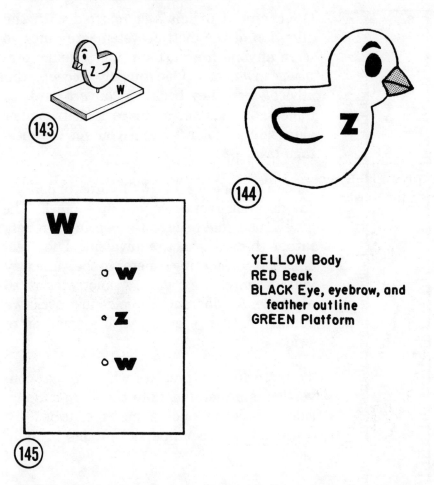

YELLOW Body
RED Beak
BLACK Eye, eyebrow, and
   feather outline
GREEN Platform

Follow decorating procedures previously outlined. Sandpaper all edges and surfaces smooth, then apply a primer before tracing outlines.

HOW TO THINK METRIC

Government officials concerned with the adoption of the metric system are quick to warn anyone from attempting to make precise conversions. One quickly accepts this advice when they begin to convert yards to meters or vice versa. Place a metric ruler alongside a foot ruler and you get the message fast.

Since a meter equals 1.09361 yards, or 39⅜″ +, the decimals can drive you up a creek. The government men suggest accepting a rough, rather than an exact equivalent. They recommend considering a meter in the same way you presently use a yard. A kilometer as 0.6 of a mile. A kilogram or kilo as just over two pounds. A liter, a quart, with a small extra swig.

To more fully appreciate why a rough conversion is preferable, note the 6″ rule alongside the metric rule. A meter contains 100 centimeters. A centimeter contains 10 millimeters.

As an introduction to the metric system, we used a metric rule to measure standard U.S. building materials. Since a 1x2 measures anywhere from ¾ to ²⁵⁄₃₂ x 1½″, which is typical of U.S. lumber sizes, the metric equivalents shown are only approximate.

Consider 1″ equal to 2.54 centimeters;
10″ = 25.4 cm.
To multiply 4¼″ into centimeters: 4.25 × 2.54 = 10.795 or 10.8 cm.

EASY-TO-USE-METRIC SCALE

DECIMAL EQUIVALENTS

1/32		.03125
	1/16	.0625
3/32		.09375
	1/8	.125
5/32		.15625
	3/16	.1875
7/32		.21875
	1/4	.250
9/32		.28125
	5/16	.3125
11/32		.34375
	3/8	.375
13/32		.40625
	7/16	.4375
15/32		.46875
	1/2	.500
17/32		.53125
	9/16	.5625
19/32		.59375
	5/8	.625
21/32		.65625
	11/16	.6875
23/32		.71875
	3/4	.750
25/32		.78125
	13/16	.8125
27/32		.84375
	7/8	.875
29/32		.90625
	15/16	.9375
31/32		.96875

FRACTIONS — CENTIMETERS

1/16		0.16
	1/8	0.32
3/16		0.48
	1/4	0.64
5/16		0.79
	3/8	0.95
7/16		1.11
	1/2	1.27
9/16		1.43
	5/8	1.59
11/16		1.75
	3/4	1.91

13/16		2.06
	7/8	2.22
15/16		2.38

INCHES — CENTIMETERS

1		2.54
	1/8	2.9
	1/4	3.2
	3/8	3.5
	1/2	3.8
	5/8	4.1
	3/4	4.4
	7/8	4.8
2		5.1
	1/8	5.4
	1/4	5.7
	3/8	6.0
	1/2	6.4
	5/8	6.7
	3/4	7.0
	7/8	7.3
3		7.6
	1/8	7.9
	1/4	8.3
	3/8	8.6
	1/2	8.9
	5/8	9.2
	3/4	9.5
	7/8	9.8
4		10.2
	1/8	10.5
	1/4	10.8
	3/8	11.1
	1/2	11.4
	5/8	11.7
	3/4	12.1
	7/8	12.4
5		12.7
	1/8	13.0
	1/4	13.3
	3/8	13.7
	1/2	14.0
	5/8	14.3
	3/4	14.6
	7/8	14.9

6		15.2
	1/8	15.6
	1/4	15.9
	3/8	16.2
	1/2	16.5
	5/8	16.8
	3/4	17.1
	7/8	17.5
7		17.8
	1/8	18.1
	1/4	18.4
	3/8	18.7
	1/2	19.1
	5/8	19.4
	3/4	19.7
	7/8	20.0
8		20.3
	1/8	20.6
	1/4	21.0
	3/8	21.3
	1/2	21.6
	5/8	21.9
	3/4	22.2
	7/8	22.5
9		22.9
	1/8	23.2
	1/4	23.5
	3/8	23.8
	1/2	24.1
	5/8	24.4
	3/4	24.8
	7/8	25.1
10		25.4
	1/8	25.7
	1/4	26.0
	3/8	26.4
	1/2	26.7
	5/8	27.0
	3/4	27.3
	7/8	27.6
11		27.9
	1/8	28.3
	1/4	28.6
	3/8	28.9
	1/2	29.2
	5/8	29.5
	3/4	29.8
	7/8	30.2

12		30.5
	1/8	30.8
	1/4	31.1
	3/8	31.4
	1/2	31.8
	5/8	32.1
	3/4	32.4
	7/8	32.7
14		35.6
16		40.6
20		50.8
30		76.2
40		101.6
50		127.0
60		152.4
70		177.8
80		203.2
90		228.6
100		254.0

FEET —	INCHES —	CENTIMETERS
1	12	30.5
2	24	61.0
3	36	91.4
4	48	121.9
5	60	152.4
6	72	182.9
7	84	213.4
8	96	243.8
9	108	274.3
10	120	304.8
11	132	335.3
12	144	365.8
13	156	396.2
14	168	426.7
15	180	457.2
16	192	487.7
17	204	518.2
18	216	548.6
19	228	579.1
20	240	609.6